VOTE FOR PRESIDENT JOHNSON
ON NOVEMBER 3.

DAISY

Also by Sean Devine

Re:Union (2013)

DAISY

a play by

SEAN DEVINE

Talonbooks

Talonbooks
278 East First Avenue, Vancouver, British Columbia, Canada V5T 1A6
www.talonbooks.com

First printing: 2017

Typeset in Arno
Printed and bound in Canada on 100% post-consumer recycled paper

Cover and interior design by Typesmith
Cover image *French Nuclear Test Licorne* courtesy Alamy Stock Photo
Cover image *Daisy* by Jay Erickson via Flickr (CC by 2.0)
Interior *Daisy* ad images courtesy of the Library of Congress

Talonbooks acknowledges the financial support of the Canada Council for the Arts, the Government of Canada through the Canada Book Fund, and the Province of British Columbia through the British Columbia Arts Council and the Book Publishing Tax Credit.

Rights to produce *Daisy*, in whole or in part, in any medium by any group, amateur or professional, are retained by the author. Interested persons are requested to contact Catherine Mensour at Mensour Agency, 41 Springfield Road, Ottawa, Ontario, Canada K1M 1C8; TELEPHONE: 613-241-1677; EMAIL: kate@mensour.ca

LIBRARY AND ARCHIVES CANADA CATALOGUING IN PUBLICATION

Devine, Sean, 1970–, author
    Daisy / a play by Sean Devine ; foreword by Joe Slade White ; introduction by Warren Kinsella.

ISBN 978-1-77201-185-2 (SOFTCOVER)

I. White, Joe Slade, writer of foreword II. Kinsella, Warren, 1960–, writer of introduction III. Title.

PS8607.E9454D35 2017   C812'.6   C2017-906002-3

For Alexa

Advertising is tax deductible.
So we all pay for the privilege of
being manipulated and controlled.

—Noam Chomsky

FOREWORD xi
by Joe Slade White

INTRODUCTION xv
by Warren Kinsella

PLAYWRIGHT'S NOTE xix
by Sean Devine

PRODUCTION HISTORY xxiii
DESIGN NOTE xxiv
CHARACTERS xxv

ACT I 1
ACT II 91

ACKNOWLEDGMENTS 159
NOTES 161

Foreword

Sean Devine has written a powerful play about a remarkable moment in history – a moment so decisive that one 60-second television commercial could determine the direction of a country. To this day, that commercial, the "Daisy" spot, is studied, argued over, and talked about 53 years after it aired – just once.

The play is *Daisy*.

One of the play's central characters is a man named Tony Schwartz. I knew the *real* Tony.

Tony Schwartz was a genius. And yes, that word gets thrown around a lot. As the joke goes, "If your hairdresser is a genius, where does that leave Mozart?" But Tony was a genius. There was always a sense, when you were with him, of the questions and theories that were swirling around in his mind. It felt as if some floodgate was barely holding back the ideas and puzzles that delighted him. And they would spill out with wonderful energy.

Tony was human. He could be irascible. He could be impatient with those who refused to listen or who didn't want to understand. He was turning communications theory upside down. And there were a lot of people who didn't like that. But Tony was also as gentle a soul as anyone I've ever met.

Tony was agoraphobic. As far as Tony was concerned, in a perfect world, he would never have stepped outside his house or, at the very least, left the familiarity of his own New York City neighbourhood. Anywhere beyond that, there were dragons.

He would walk. He literally invented the portable tape recorder so he could walk through his neighbourhood, recording all of its sounds – its reality – and his.

I had bragging rights to say I'd actually walked down a city street with Tony. We left his house and walked two blocks. And then we walked back. I can remember every step. And Tony would have too. He was listening. He was always listening.

I remember Tony once admonished me for believing the rumour that he had never left Manhattan. "I left once," he said to me. Then he added, "I won't do *that* again." And I'm pretty sure he didn't.

In 1964, the team from Doyle Dane Bernbach (DDB), which was in charge of advertising for President Lyndon Johnson's election campaign, came to Tony's home and studio in Hell's Kitchen. They were seeking Tony's help. Some didn't think they needed it. Tony gave them a brilliant idea and a road map to create what is now considered the most powerful political ad ever made.

There have always been differences over who did what to produce that ad. But if anyone could do a DNA test on the "Daisy" ad, Tony Schwartz's DNA is all over it. The use of a child's voice; the innocent and hesitant count of the daisy petals, turning into the ominous male voice's countdown, and most of all, the use of Tony's unique "resonance theory." [1]

The "Daisy" ad played just one time, yet its effect on the Barry Goldwater campaign was devastating. It touched a true chord in the American public that was already there. It elicited a response against Goldwater's admitted potential use of nuclear weapons in the Vietnam War, without needing to mention Goldwater's name.

Tony's "resonance theory" held that the message of any commercial is created by the audience, not the commercial itself. In the "Daisy" commercial, presidential candidate Barry Goldwater is never mentioned. Tony told me that if Goldwater's name been spoken the spot would have not worked. Instead, Tony understood the audience would create the message themselves and fill in the name.

In his play *Daisy*, Sean Devine has pulled off something that seems effortless, but in fact is extremely rare and hard to do. Devine has written characters that actually existed in history.

---

[1] "Resonance theory" – sometimes referred to as "resonance principle," "resonance model," or "responsive chord" – may be further explored in Tony Schwartz's *The Responsive Chord* (1973) and multiple sources online.

That's never easy, and hard to do well. Yet these characters come to life, ring true, and make us want to hear more.

It's history. We know how it all turns out. Yet this playwright makes us want to find out how it all turns out. That's a bit of magic. And why we go to the theatre. And why we read plays.

Each time I read the play and come across one of Tony's lines, I say to myself, "Yes. That's Tony. That's exactly what Tony would say and how he would sound." And that's not at all easy to accomplish.

I'm grateful and honoured to have this opportunity to give back something of what Tony meant to me. I'm proud of my reputation for having trained a great number of the next generation of Democratic media consultants, and that is due to what Tony did for me, and how he taught me.

Have fun. It's a good story.

—JOE SLADE WHITE
East Aurora, New York, 2017

Introduction

In politics, as in life, everyone thinks they are an expert at communications. So every political hack thinks they're an expert at making political commercials, too.

They're not, of course, but that doesn't stop them from trying. So, there were the Paul Martin Liberals in Canada, with their 2006 ad that falsely claimed that the Conservatives planned to institute "[s]oldiers with guns. In our cities. In Canada."[1] That one helped contribute to Martin's defeat, his promised "juggernaut"[2] rendered a joke, his government now a footnote.

And then there were the Kim Campbell Conservatives, also in Canada, with their 1993 ad that mocked Liberal leader Jean Chrétien's facial paralysis, asking, "Is this a Prime Minister?"[3] That one accelerated Campbell's defeat, reducing the majority Conservative government to two seats.

In the U.S., perhaps one of the most notoriously bad political commercials of all time was Christine O'Donnell's contribution to the genre in 2010. O'Donnell was running for the Senate in the state of Delaware and decided to broadcast an ad in which she said – straight to camera – that she was "not a witch."[4] There is a reason why political candidates are always advised never to repeat a negative. O'Donnell's ad does that – and it helped her to lose in a spectacular fashion.

Then there was the 2016 presidential campaign, during which my wife and I – full disclosure – volunteered for Hillary Clinton.

---

[1] To view the full ad, refer to: https://youtu.be/uMsqEph7a8I

[2] Delacourt, Susan. *Juggernaut: Paul Martin's campaign for Chrétien's crown.* Toronto: McClelland & Stewart, 2003.

[3] A quote from the ad, which may be viewed here: https://youtu.be/DoooAmn9CIA

[4] To view the full ad, refer to: https://youtu.be/ek3OUay2uWw

Clinton's campaign ran no shortage of advertising about how Trump had made offensive and racist statements. What they didn't do, however, is what "Daisy" did – broadcast an ad that reminded Americans why Trump's temperament made him wholly unsuited for the office of president.

Everyone knew he was a racist before he was a candidate. What they didn't know, and what they needed to be reminded of, was that he was precisely the sort of man who would plunge the world into unwanted wars.

So, not everyone is good at this political ad stuff.

On one thing everyone – experts and non-experts alike – can usually agree, however. The best political ad was "Daisy."

It was (and is) without equal. It is the one that is the greatest. The matchless one. The one *nonpareil.* Peerless, primo, perfect.

As in all things political, its parentage is claimed by many. "Victory has many fathers," John F. Kennedy famously said, "but defeat is an orphan."

The guy most consider to be the one who came up with the *idea* behind "Daisy," if not every bit of it, was a New York City sound guy named Tony Schwartz. He had an idea, he once told me, of a little girl in a field somewhere, plucking the petals off a daisy, counting, in a little girl's sing-song voice. Countdown to a bomb. That's it, pretty much.

I told Schwartz that everyone agrees his political ad was the best ever made, the one that made history – running just once (once!) and contributing to Lyndon B. Johnson's landslide victory over Barry Goldwater in the 1964 presidential race. But I also told him that not everyone agrees about *why* it worked. Did it touch their hearts? Their minds? Their hopes and dreams and fears? Why did it work so powerfully? Why do we still speak of it, in such reverent tones, a half-century after it aired for the first and only time?

Tony Schwartz was a quiet old fellow when I spoke to him, an agoraphobic. He didn't like to go outside his home. He was impressed, he allowed, that someone from far-away Canada knew who he was, and wanted to speak to him.

Why did "Daisy" work?

He thought for a minute. "A political ad is about things that are important to the people, at the time election is taking place," he said. "Daisy" came out when Goldwater had been openly musing about using nuclear weapons against America's enemies. Said Schwartz: "When the commercial came on, people asked themselves, 'Whose finger do I want on the nuclear trigger? The man who wants to use them, or the man who doesn't?'"

"Daisy" was about choices, then. Every election is about choices, when distilled down to its base elements. But "Daisy" was about more than that, too. It was about something deeper.

In our interview, Schwartz came close to explaining what, exactly, "Daisy" did. But he explains it best in his book *The Responsive Chord*. Wrote Schwartz: "The best political commercials are similar to Rorschach patterns. They do not tell the viewer anything. They surface his feelings, and provide a context for him to express those feelings."

When you understand that the political brain is about emotion, not reason, you get closer to Schwartz's theory. When you accept that most voters make choices with their *hearts*, not their *minds*, you get his point. And you start to understand why atrocities like Donald Trump can happen.

Progressives like me always like to appeal to the intellect, to a voter's better instincts. We get tongue-tied when talking about emotion.

That is why we lose. That is why extremists like Trump triumph. Because we forget the best political ads – the best political speeches, the best political debate lines, the best political communications – are an opportunity for people to surface their feelings, as Schwartz says. The deep, deep down stuff. The stuff that is impossible to put into words, but is no less real for that.

Sean Devine came to see me, a couple years back, with an idea about *Daisy*. He shared my fascination with the ad, for Schwartz's theory, for the history that was created by that single 60-second TV spot.

He wanted to do a play about "Daisy." Being a guy who started a political consulting firm called Daisy – and who even had a chocolate lab called Daisy – I understood his enthusiasm for the subject matter.

Sean's play attempts to place "Daisy" in its larger and proper context. It doesn't hand out awards for authorship. But it accepts that – on that one night in September 1964, for just 60 seconds – the greatest bit of political communication was broadcast, and it changed *everything.*

"Daisy" did that. "Daisy" was the best. Still is. Read Sean's play and understand.

—WARREN KINSELLA
Toronto, Ontario, 2017

Playwright's Note

The commercial aired only once. And we're still talking about it.
History plays are more than reflections on our past. They shine new light on our present. And if they're based on incidents of enduring currency, if they dramatize individuals of rare genius, then our ever-shifting present will continue to be illuminated by these stories.

Early in my research, I came upon the controversy over authorship of the "Daisy" ad. It was soon clear that the controversy hadn't diminished since the spot aired in 1964. There were two camps, each fiercely defended. One claimed that Tony Schwartz was the genius and sole inspiration behind the ad. The other held the position that the "ad men" at Madison Avenue top agency Doyle Dane Bernbach were the brains behind "Daisy."

Despite the uncertainty, several things are clear. To me, at least. First, the "Daisy" ad, which was created in 1964, would not exist if it weren't for a remarkably similar radio spot that Schwartz created on his own in 1962. Second, and despite the first point, the most famous political commercial ever made was the result of a creative collaboration in which many hands played instrumental roles in its conception and execution: Tony Schwartz, Sid Myers, Stan Lee, Aaron Ehrlich, Lloyd Wright, and of course Bill Bernbach. If it weren't for each of their influences, we would not have such an incredibly nuanced and perfectly packaged spot. And third, all of these magnificent figures deserve their place in the history of modern communications.

Bill Bernbach ushered in advertising's Creative Revolution, bringing excitement and renewed appreciation to a then-tired industry that lacked in lustre and had surfeit of cynicism. The tasteful maverick whose quotes adorn the walls of ad agencies everywhere taught his leagues of offspring that, whereas advertising is persuasion, persuasion itself is not a science, but an art.

Tony Schwartz was a man ahead of his time, and though he faced restrictions of space and conventionality, he broke the barriers of each. A man of the people, he'd converse with his colleague Marshall McLuhan, or with a sitting president, or with the fruit vendor down the street. It was all of equal value. And it's all stored in the collection that bears his name at the Library of Congress.

These two giants revolutionized the way we transmit and even understand ideas and information. And they made their greatest impact at a time when our species was ill-prepared for an unstoppable wave of persuasion, delivered upon our defenseless senses through the unprecedented power of television.

The effect of electronic media, and specifically television, on politics and campaigning – the effect of television on EVERY-THING – is one of paradigm shift. Campaigns that failed to understand and incorporate these new technologies to their full potential were decimated. We've seen the same thing in recent years with campaigns that lack effective strategies for social media.

Speaking of media, it's impossible to get a true sense of the new realities described in this play without experiencing the various media elements referred to in this script. The Notes following the script contain links which are a great reference set for any reader wanting an extra-dimensional experience of the play. But I'd like to highlight some foundational elements here.

If the 1964 presidential election was the first American contest that saw the impact television commercials could have on a campaign, then it's the creative minds at Bill Bernbach's flagship agency who are responsible for that. The best place to see the whole body of their work on the 1964 campaign is at www.livingroomcandidate.org. This site includes a history of American presidential campaign commercials – Republican and Democrat – dating back to 1952. By comparing the ads that Bernbach's team created for Lyndon Johnson with Barry Goldwater's tired missives, it's easy to see their game-changing effect. And while you're there, take a look at the ads that helped propel Richard Nixon to the presidency in the 1968 campaign and demonstrate, in hindsight, just how wary we must be about the power of advertising.

Which brings me, finally, to Tony Schwartz, a man whose work still resonates throughout our heavily-mediated world. And it's hardly an exaggeration to say that his book *The Responsive Chord* is a sacred text in some circles. Though it may seem simple now, Tony's "resonance theory," derived from his understanding of the mechanics of hearing, is still a mind-blowing concept. And it's a concept that, frankly, will stand the test of time no matter where technology takes us, because nothing will outpace the electronic speed that the theory is based on.

I hope you enjoy the play, and that its arguments and discoveries are as relevant now as they were in 1964. I hope the story resonates.

Or as Tony might say, I hope you remember it for the rest of your …

—SEAN DEVINE
Ottawa, Ontario, 2017

PRODUCTION HISTORY

Daisy had its world premiere on July 14, 2016, at ACT –
A Contemporary Theatre in Seattle, Washington, under John
Langs, Artistic Director, with the following company:

LOUISE BROWN	Kirsten Potter
TONY SCHWARTZ	Michael Gotch
CLIFFORD LEWIS	Tré Cotten
BILL BERNBACH	R. Hamilton Wright
SID MYERS	Connor Toms
AARON EHRLICH	Bradford Farwell

Director	John Langs
Scenic Designer	Shawn Ketchum Johnson
Lighting Designer	Robert J. Aguilar
Video/Projections designer	Tristan Roberson
Sound Designer	Robertson Witmer
Stage Manager	JR Welden

Daisy was developed in part at the Icicle Creek New Play
Festival under Allen Fitzpatrick, Artistic Director. *Daisy* was
also developed in part by Horseshoes & Hand Grenades
Theatre and originally commissioned by The Ensemble
Studio Theatre / Alfred P. Sloan Foundation Science &
Technology Project.

DESIGN NOTE

For the original production of *Daisy* at Seattle's ACT, directed by John Langs, the central focus for the set design was a massive upstage wall consisting of dozens of television screens, onto which was projected any number of orientations of the play's many video elements. The remaining physical elements were minimal but highly functional, allowing for the scenes to shift quickly between numerous locations. Three wooden desks and two movable wooden benches represented the large workspace at ad agency Doyle Dane Bernbach. The centre desk served as the main console in Tony Schwartz's studio, with a shelving unit upstage of the desk. (For the Seattle production, the shelving unit was able to rise up from the floor thanks to a marvelous hydraulic lift, but few productions will be able to pull that off!) Each of the desks and benches had drawers and compartments – some obvious, some custom-built – which allowed for props to appear and disappear with ease. Other scenic elements were brought in from the wings or the fly system as needed.

As mentioned above, the script has numerous references to projection as well as sound elements, and these elements will be instrumental for any production of *Daisy*. For this publication, we've tried to be as descriptive as possible to give the reader a sense of what's happening, using the terms *PROJECTION* and *SOUND* with any relevant stage directions.

CHARACTERS

LOUISE (LOU) BROWN
    Late thirties. A copywriter with the advertising firm of
    Doyle Dane Bernbach.

TONY SCHWARTZ
    Early forties. A sound archivist, media specialist,
    and agoraphobe.

CLIFFORD (CLIFF) LEWIS
    Early thirties. African-American. A White House lawyer.

BILL BERNBACH
    Early fifties. The creative director of the firm that
    bears his name.

SIDNEY (SID) MYERS
    Mid-thirties. An art director with Doyle Dane Bernbach.

AARON EHRLICH
    Early forties. A television producer with Doyle
    Dane Bernbach.

Other supporting characters appear in various forms.

ACT I

PROLOGUE

*PROJECTION: A montage of television footage
reveals snippets of history and commercialism
which bring us back to the years just prior to 1964.
Kennedy and Nixon squared off on televised debate.
Kindergarten students learning to duck and cover
under their desks. Water cannons discharging on
black Alabamans. A limo speeding away in Dallas.
A dutiful Vice-President being sworn in.*

*Blending into this, ad after ad make their pitch for
products that are better, faster, sharper, stronger,
cleaner and leaner than all the rest.*

*And then it all disappears into darkness and
near quiet.*

ACT I | SCENE 1

From the dark, a voice speaks.

TONY

Hello? Are we ready to begin? Does everyone have a seat? …
How do I sound? Do I sound close? It doesn't feel close.
Let's adjust that.

*A light comes up on TONY SCHWARTZ. He's giving
a lecture. Beside him is a tape player.*

TONY

1, 2, 3. Comunication. Partipulation. That's better. Let's
begin … Hello, everyone. I'm honoured to be speaking to
you all today. My name is Tony Schwartz. If there's a subject
I can speak about with some level of expertise, it would
be the area of sound. Of closeness. We had our earliest
experience of closeness through sound.

TONY turns on the tape player.

SOUND: A slow, regular heartbeat.

TONY

The sound of our mother's heartbeat.

Another heartbeat blends in with the first, faster.

TONY

Of our own heartbeat. We developed our sense of rhythm
through these two heartbeats playing in counterpoint. Our first
communication was hearing speech inside the womb, resonating
through bone and water conduction. Long before you could see
the difference between a smile or a frown, you could hear the
difference in the sound of a word. In the sound of anger. The
sound of love. The sound of fear.

TONY stops the tape player.

TONY

There was a composer who performed an experiment on the nature of silence. He placed himself inside an "anechoic chamber," which is a room without echoes. A room without sound. But inside the chamber, the composer heard two sounds. One high. And one low.

TONY starts another playback.

SOUND: Two frequencies, one high and one low.

TONY

He asks the technician, "Why, if the room is silent, do I hear those two sounds? One high, and one low." The composer is told that the high frequency is his nervous system in operation. The low frequency is his blood in circulation.

TONY stops the tape player.

Even when we are quiet, there's no such thing as silence. Even when we are lonely, there's no such thing as empty space. The vastness of human consciousness is a bottomless well that we as communicators can draw from. Can you *see* what I am saying?

ACT I | SCENE 2

A work room inside the New York City advertising agency Doyle Dane Bernbach.

SID MYERS is pitching an idea to LOUISE BROWN. SID stands in front of an easel with a product board. It shows the logo for American Airlines.

SID

Now, if we are going to succeed in making American Airlines stand out from all other airlines, then it behooves us to ask what is it about air travel in general that begs improvement. And can we change it? Can we change the fact that you're in a fart-filled steel box for five hours? No. Can we change the fact that sometimes you get stuck next to the crying baby? No, we cannot. But what we can change, what American Airlines can offer is that one special person who invites the customer to "fly away with me."

LOUISE

(*teasing*) You mean the pilot.

SID

The stewardess! It's a known fact. It is practically science: men have a natural attraction to stewardesses.

LOUISE

That's science, huh?

SID

I have three college friends who married stewardesses.

LOUISE

How many of them are still married?

SID

    One, and they have a beautiful relationship.

        *AARON EHRLICH enters with a book. He always
        wears dark-tinted glasses.*

AARON

    Sid, I'm telling you, you've got to read this book.
    It's terrifying.

SID

    Aaron, I'm in the middle of something.

AARON

    I'm on the chapter where it describes how the Soviets have
    targeted our cities.

SID

    I don't want to hear about that book. Now if you don't mind.

AARON

    Don't we have a meeting with Mr. Bernbach?

SID

    He's on his way.

AARON

    Did he say what the meeting's for?

SID

    No.

AARON

    Whatever it is, it's big. The corridors are buzzing.

SID

    Aaron, I'm trying to pitch an idea on Lou.

AARON

So she can turn around and make it better?

SID

Hey! (*to LOUISE*) Lou, how long do you think the career of
a stewardess is?

AARON

(*reading from book*) "In Alabama's bigger cities, like
Birmingham, the Soviets would be hit with ten megatons."
Why so many megatons?

SID

The average career of a stewardess is two years. Do you
know why it's only two years?

AARON

Because they marry the customers.

SID

Because they marry the customers.

AARON

"But in Alabama's smaller cities like Tuscaloosa, the Soviets
would hit with only half a megaton."

LOUISE

(*to SID*) So what's your pitch, Sid?

AARON

(*flipping pages, nervous*) What's it say about New York?

LOUISE

American Airlines starts offering weddings on trans-
Atlantic flights?

SID

You got a better angle? Be my guest.

LOUISE

Right, so you can tell Bernbach it's yours.

SID

What's that supposed to mean?

AARON

(*referring to the book*) Aw, geez. New York's going to be hit with a hundred megatons. My wife's going to lose it.

LOUISE

I know how things work, Sid. A bunch of ideas get tossed around. You put in your two cents. I put in a nickel. All of a sudden, you're walking around with seven cents.

AARON

You should've heard Vera when she read about radiation burns. I thought only bats could hit that frequency.

SID

Aaron, if you don't shut up about that book –

LOUISE

What's this book?

AARON

(*giving it to her*) Lou, you got to read this. It's important.

SID

It's depressing.

LOUISE

(*reading the title*) "Strategy for Survival: A Comprehensive Account of Thermonuclear War."

SID

(*to AARON*) I'm surprised Vera sleeps with you.

AARON

Vera's the one who bought it. She's more scared than I
am. I'm the voice of reason. When is Mr. Bernbach going
to get here?

SID

Stop acting so nervous!

AARON

I can't help it. He's intimidating.

LOUISE

Mr. Bernbach's not intimidating. He's formidable. Just don't
disappoint him.

AARON

I don't think Mr. Bernbach likes me. He always looks at me
like I'm peculiar.

SID

Maybe it's the glasses.

AARON

They're prescription! I've got a condition!

SID

So, Lou, what do you think the meeting's for? Betcha five
bucks it's a merger.

LOUISE

Five bucks. That's dinner and a movie.

SID

Dinner and a movie wouldn't cost anything if you had
someone paying for it.

AARON

I'll tell you what the meeting's about. I think I'm
getting fired.

SID

What?

AARON

The writing's on the wall. If only it wasn't so blurry.

SID

For crying out loud. That book's got you paranoid.

AARON

Reality's got me paranoid. Remember Cuba? Reality almost
ceased to exist.

SID

(*to AARON*) Enough with the life and death. You're worse
than my daughter. Kid's in second grade, this morning at
breakfast she's practicing how to duck and cover.

LOUISE

(*to herself*) It's about life and death.

SID

What is?

LOUISE

It's about living. No. It's about not dying. You're right, Sid.
We make it about the man on the plane. The one who falls
for the stewardess. It's about him.

> LOUISE *goes up to the product board.*

He's been taking this flight a few years now. Two, three
times a month. Same business trip. Same destination. The
same stewardess. Beautiful girl. Bright as the sun. The kind

of girl that makes a man think about all the choices he's made. She calls him by his first name. She puts her hand on his shoulder in a way that's just perfect. She always smiles, no matter what's happening. Even when she's scared. And when he gets off the plane, when he passes her by on his way out the door, that's his chance. He wants to smile, he wants to let her know, but all he can say is "Thank you." Because just off the plane, just past the door, there's his wife, and there's his little girl. And they're his whole world. And he's just so happy that he got home safe.

SID
(*after a moment*) Fine. If you want to do it sentimental.

AARON
I think I'm gonna call Vera.

> CLIFFORD LEWIS, *in a suit, enters. He has an envelope.*

CLIFFORD
Excuse me, I'm looking for Mr. Ehrlich, Mr. Myers –

AARON
You want me to sign for something?

CLIFFORD
I'm sorry?

AARON
What do you want me to sign? (*looking him over*) They wearing suits in the mail room now?

CLIFFORD
(*to AARON*) Are you Myers?

SID
I'm Sid Myers. That's Aaron Ehrlich.

CLIFFORD
I've got a meeting with the two of you.

AARON
You've got a meeting with us?

CLIFFORD
And a Mr. Brown.

SID
(*teasing*) Mr. Brown?

CLIFFORD
Mr. L. Brown.

LOUISE
You mean Louise Brown.

CLIFFORD
Oh. I didn't –

AARON
What are you meeting with us for?

CLIFFORD
I'll let Mr. Bernbach explain.

AARON
Mr. Bernbach?

LOUISE
Won't you come in, Mister ...

CLIFFORD
Lewis. Clifford Lewis.

> *BILL BERNBACH enters.*
> *AARON doesn't see him.*

AARON

You're meeting with Mr. Bernbach? Alright, now. Someone better tell me what's going on. Because, frankly, I'm starting to get irritated.

BERNBACH

And what is it you find irritating, Aaron?

AARON

Mr. Bernbach, I didn't hear you come in.

BERNBACH

You made that clear.

AARON

When I said I was irritated, Mr. Bernbach, I was referring to my eyes, sir. I have a condition. They get irritated. I have bug eyes, Mr. Bernbach. That's why I wear the glasses. I only take them off at home. My wife's very forgiving.

BERNBACH

She'd have to be. (*turning to* CLIFFORD) Clifford, I'm sorry if I kept you waiting. I trust my staff was hospitable.

CLIFFORD

Yes, sir.

BERNBACH

May I introduce Clifford Lewis? Sidney Myers is a senior art director.

SID

(*shaking hands*) Hey there, Clifford.

BERNBACH

Aaron Ehrlich, one of our producers. And Louise Brown, one of our top copywriters.

CLIFFORD
(*shaking hands*) Hello.

LOUISE
Hello.

BERNBACH
Are those the contracts?

CLIFFORD
They are.

> CLIFFORD *hands the envelope to* BERNBACH,
> *who takes out contracts.*

BERNBACH
How was the train up from Washington?

CLIFFORD
Very pleasant.

SID
So what's going on, Mr. Bernbach?

BERNBACH
(*to* CLIFFORD) You're a lawyer, Clifford, is that right?

CLIFFORD
Yes, sir.

AARON
(*ruefully*) Aw, geez.

BERNBACH
(*to* CLIFFORD) But more specifically ...

CLIFFORD
I'm the White House Deputy Special Counsel.

SID
   Oh, baby.

AARON
   (*even more so*) Aw, geez.

SID
   Alright, sir, you've got our attention. What's this about?

BERNBACH
   It's about change, Sidney. Fundamental change.

   BERNBACH signs the contracts.

BERNBACH
   Our firm may not be the biggest. It might not pay as well as
   the competition. But there's currency to prestige. Clifford
   was recently tasked by the White House to choose an
   advertising firm. Thanks to his recommendation, I just
   signed a contract making us the agency of record to help
   Lyndon Johnson become our next President.

   SID, AARON, and LOUISE erupt in jubilation.

AARON
   Are you kidding me?

SID
   Oh, baby!

AARON
   Are you kidding me?!

SID
   (*to CLIFFORD*) That's some poker face.

CLIFFORD
Mr. Bernbach put me up to it.

AARON
The President?

BERNBACH
Yes, Aaron.

AARON
Are you kidding me?!

LOUISE
(*to BERNBACH*) This is huge, Mr. Bernbach.

SID
Huge? This is the Alps!

BERNBACH
Before we celebrate, let's be clear on what we're getting
into. This is our first-ever political campaign. It will have an
impact on us all. The workload will be grueling. There will
be about thirty of you on the account, which is to be your
only focus from now until November 3rd. All other accounts
will be handed to other staff. The three of you, with Clifford
as your liaison, are in charge of television advertising.

SID
Oh, baby!

AARON
Are you kidding me?!

SID
(*to AARON*) How you feeling now, huh? You paranoid
little freak.

AARON

I'm feeling pretty good! Unlike the poor schmucks *not* on
the account.

BERNBACH

I've only ever hired one or two schmucks, Aaron.

AARON

What I meant was how grateful I am, for the privilege.
I mean, how'd you decide who's on board? Was it seniority?
Did you pick names out of a hat?

CLIFFORD

You can't be a Republican.

        Pause.

SID

What was that?

CLIFFORD

There can't be any Republicans on the account. It's in
the contract.

SID

Wow.

LOUISE

Mr. Bernbach, is that true?

BERNBACH

It's not something I'd normally approve, but –

LOUISE

If this were Marlboro, would you be checking which of us
smoked Lucky Strikes?

BERNBACH

This is new ground, Louise. The client made the request, and I've accepted it. I chose the three of you because my observations and some gentle inquiries lead me to believe you're all Democrats. If I'm wrong, now would be a good time to correct me.

SID

Heck, I got mouths to feed. Even if I was Republican, I'd tear up my card for this. But I was a Democrat before Kennedy and I ain't changing anytime soon.

AARON

Back in college, I had a threesome with two Republican girls. That's the closest I came to switching sides.

BERNBACH

Louise?

LOUISE

I'm a Democrat, sir.

BERNBACH

Then it's settled. Sidney, I'd like you to show Clifford some Doyle Dane Bernbach hospitality.

SID

You got it.

CLIFFORD

And next week I'll show you around Washington. Starting with the White House.

AARON

The White House! Are you kidding me?! ... But that's a five-hundred-megaton target.

SID

We'll set you up in the presidential bunker. Let's go, boys.
I know a couple joints that will blow your mind.

> CLIFF and AARON exit,
> with SID and LOUISE trailing.

BERNBACH

Louise, may I speak to you?

LOUISE

(*to* SID) I'll catch up with you.

SID

(*hesitant*) Sure. We'll be down at the –

LOUISE

Yeah.

> SID exits.

LOUISE

This is great news, Mr. Bernbach. It's historic.

BERNBACH

It's a far cry from selling ketchup.

LOUISE

I'll say. I'm flattered you chose me, sir.

BERNBACH

You're more than worthy of the assignment, Louise.

LOUISE

You know, you can call me "Lou," like the fellas do.

BERNBACH
My doorman's name is "Lou." Would you prefer I associate you with my doorman?

LOUISE
No, sir.

BERNBACH
This firm was built on principles. Creativity, good taste, and above all integrity. I see all of those in you. You're an extraordinary talent. There aren't many firms that would encourage a woman to go as far as I believe you can go. (*pausing*) Television has come to politics. And so politics has come to us. It will change everything we do. I won't allow it to change who we are. I'm counting on you for that.

LOUISE
I'll do my best, sir.

BERNBACH
Your best is more than enough. Now go join your friends.

> *LOUISE doesn't move.*

BERNBACH
Yes?

LOUISE
You remind me of someone.

BERNBACH
Ah. I hope he's very dashing.

LOUISE
He is. You remind me of my father.

BERNBACH
I see. I'll try to take that as a compliment.

LOUISE
You should.

BERNBACH
Then I will. He's a hero of yours?

LOUISE
He's one of them.

She leaves.

ACT I | SCENE 3

PROJECTION (text): April 1964

CLIFFORD's basement office at the White House.
A meeting between CLIFFORD, LOUISE, SID
and AARON.

At the front is a chalkboard. On one side, below a
photograph of NELSON ROCKEFELLER:
   "Rockefeller Issues: i) Winning the South,
   ii) Entitlement, iii) Family Trouble"

On the other side, below a photograph
of BARRY GOLDWATER:
   "Goldwater Issues: i) Social Security,
   ii) Recklessness, iii) Nuclear Responsibility"

CLIFFORD

Now the way I see it, the closer we match advertising
to campaign strategy, the greater chance for a
winning campaign.

AARON

Vera won't believe this. I'm inside the White House. The
basement, but still.

CLIFFORD

The strategy is a two-pronged assault, which we want to see
replicated in the advertising.

AARON

You see all the things they've got with the White House
symbol? Even the ashtrays.

CLIFFORD

First, promote President Johnson. His accomplishments
as well as what lies ahead. Second, attack and degrade
our opponent.

AARON

Cliff, do you get to take home all these things with the
White House symbol on them?

CLIFFORD

No. Now, obviously, we won't know our opponent until the
Republican convention in July.

SID

Three months. No problem.

CLIFFORD

As for President Johnson: next month the White House
announces a major social program.

SID

What's the name?

CLIFFORD

I can tell you, but keep it under wraps until we go public. It's
called the Great Society.

SID

Good name. What's the objective?

CLIFFORD

The elimination of poverty and racial injustice.

SID

Is that all?

LOUISE

So, when Johnson signs the Civil Rights Act in July,
I presume that's front and centre in this Great Society.

CLIFFORD

Absolutely.

LOUISE

Well, there's a spot right there.

CLIFFORD

What's a spot?

SID

She means an advertisement. A spot's an ad.

LOUISE

We start on the President signing the Civil Rights Act. Then
we're in a classroom. A college. A young white man has his
hand up. He's answering a question. And right next to him,
a young black man has his hand up, too.

AARON

That's a spot, alright.

CLIFFORD

I can see why Mr. Bernbach put you on the account, Miss
Brown. Now, as for our opponent. Our likeliest offensive will
be against Governor Nelson Rockefeller, but Senator Barry
Goldwater is definitely giving him a run for his money.

LOUISE

Speaking of money, not only will Rockefeller definitely be
the nominee –

AARON

I don't know, Lou. This Goldwater …

LOUISE

(*pushing through*) But when it comes to advertising,
Rockefeller's deep pockets will have him out-spending
Johnson five-to-one.

CLIFFORD

Which brings us to the specific issues we'd target for
opposition attacks.

LOUISE

Clifford, you spend any time in the military? You've got a
flair for forceful language.

> *AARON laughs. CLIFFORD holds up a piece of*
> *chalk: a challenge.*

CLIFFORD
Mr. Ehrlich.

> *AARON goes to the board.*

AARON

For Rockefeller, what you've got here seems clear to
me. "Winning the South." The President's from Texas.
Rockefeller's an Eastern elite. Can't imagine many
Alabamans lining up to shake his hand.

CLIFFORD
Mr. Myers.

> *SID replaces AARON at the board, and takes*
> *the chalk.*

SID

"Entitlement." Rockefeller's so filthy rich he can't relate to
the common man. As for "Family Trouble" ... Well, you can't
buy your way out of the kind of trouble he's in.

AARON
   Not after that divorce.

LOUISE
   Aaron!

CLIFFORD
   (*to* SID) Keep going.

SID
   It's not the divorce that cost him. It's the price tag on getting
   remarried. The political price tag.

LOUISE
   Guys!

AARON
   It's his own fault. The man was sneaking around with the
   new bride while still married to the old bride.

SID
   I hear the new bride might be expecting.

AARON
   And people count back nine months ...

LOUISE
   Could we show some respect, please?

CLIFFORD
   I don't recall asking anyone to wear white gloves, Miss
   Brown. Now, on to Goldwater. The Senator's on record
   saying that Social Security should be made voluntary. That's
   an easy target for an attack ad. As for "Recklessness" –

AARON
   The guy's a loose cannon. Some of the things he says.

CLIFFORD

Which brings us to "Nuclear Responsibility." In the unlikely scenario that Goldwater becomes the nominee, this is where we hit him.

AARON

I should've brought some Mylanta.

CLIFFORD

Obviously, there'd be less ammunition on this issue if it comes to Rockefeller, but he's still a hawk. What we need to focus on is: people are afraid of the Bomb. We all remember Cuba.

AARON

Hell, yes! Now there's the situation in Vietnam.

SID

You can't compare Cuba and Vietnam. Cuba was a fiasco.

CLIFFORD

And the nation is afraid because of it. The message we need to communicate is that Lyndon Johnson is the only sane option in a world that's come too close to insanity.

LOUISE

Clifford, how much time do you want us to spend on Barry Goldwater? He's not a contender.

AARON

The guy's got a following. That book of his, it's a bestseller.

LOUISE

So was *Mein Kampf*.

CLIFFORD

We're preparing for either scenario. Whoever the Republicans nominate, we want him on defense from the start. Especially on the nuclear issue. If it's Rockefeller, we might have to dig. But if it's Goldwater, every single voter needs to know what's at stake. Do we elect a responsible, peaceful man like Lyndon Johnson? Or do we elect a reckless individual who could easily take us into a nuclear war?

AARON
You sold me!

LOUISE
That's some pretty muscular rhetoric.

CLIFFORD
Elections don't get won on weak rhetoric.

LOUISE
You're making it sound like Goldwater would start a war. Don't you think that's a little irresponsible?

SID
Easy, Lou.

CLIFFORD
What we're looking to create, Miss Brown, is a state of urgency.

LOUISE
Sounds more like a state of fear.

CLIFFORD
Fear produces paralysis. Urgency motivates action. The reason we wish to create urgency is because the campaign might lack tension.

SID
(*after a moment*) I'm sorry, you want to increase tension?

CLIFFORD

In the polls we've conducted, the President leads both his Republican rivals by wide margins. A lack of tension will keep a lot of Democrats home on election day. We'd win, but not by enough.

LOUISE

The President wants a landslide.

CLIFFORD

The Great Society isn't going to come easy.

LOUISE

So this is why you want us to do – What did you call them, attack ads? You want us to go on the attack.

CLIFFORD

We didn't hire you to praise our opponent.

LOUISE

No. You hired us to sell a product, which is the President of the United –

CLIFFORD

(*speaking over*) Please do not refer to the President as a product.

SID

What Louise means is we highlight the positive –

LOUISE

(*speaking over*) I can explain myself, Sid. (*to* CLIFFORD) There's a generally accepted principle in advertising, which is don't go negative. Our job is to take a product, and connect that product to a hopeful consumer by showing the product in a way that's creative, in a way that's positive. What we don't do, out of good taste but also sheer ethics, is attack the competition.

CLIFFORD
(*after a moment*) Is that how this works? You meet with the client, the client tells you what he wants, then you challenge the client's ethics?

AARON
It rarely happens this way.

CLIFFORD
I can appreciate that this is new to you, Miss Brown.

LOUISE
Yesterday I was selling ketchup. Now I'm selling a president.

CLIFFORD
And politics is a lot messier than ketchup. When we came as close to the brink as we did in Cuba, when we came face to face with the unimaginable, at the church on my street there was a lineup for confession three blocks long. At three o'clock in the morning. If we ever get that close again, I'm going to be damn sure whose hand isn't on the controls.

ACT I | SCENE 4

On the train back to New York, shortly after.
SID, AARON, and LOUISE are in mid-argument.

SID

And what I'm saying, Lou, is you don't challenge the client like that. Maybe you can afford to lose your job, but I can't. He's the goddamn White House liaison!

AARON

How long's the train back home?

SID

Two hours. (*to LOUISE*) If Mr. Bernbach heard you speak to a client like that –

LOUISE

He'd probably agree with me.

AARON

I don't know why you mentioned ketchup.

SID

(*to LOUISE*) I'm going to be straight with you.

LOUISE

Here we go.

SID

You have my utmost respect. You have my highest professional regard …

LOUISE

(*interrupting*) I know where this is headed.

SID

(*pushing through*) ... but you need to step back to the curb.

LOUISE

Because I'm a woman.

SID

Because you don't know when to stay in line. You don't challenge the client on ethics. Especially when the client is the White House!

LOUISE

Then tell me. Where's the ethics in attack ads? Have you ever heard of such a thing?

SID

This isn't straight advertising, Lou. It's politics.

LOUISE

The standards should be higher *because* it's politics. We're electing a president.

AARON

Either of you two hungry?

SID

Politics is dirty. Get used to it.

LOUISE

I will not get used to it. Tell me that when Cliff was talking about attack ads, that didn't feel like a slippery slope.

SID

We've already slipped down it. Andrew Jackson and John Quincy Adams called each other pimp and adulterer in any newspaper that spared the ink.

LOUISE
In newspapers, Sid. This is television.

AARON
I could go for a sandwich.

LOUISE
There's a reason Mr. Bernbach never wanted to get us into politics. It's uncharted waters.

SID
And no one's asking you to steer the boat.

LOUISE
Someone's got to.

AARON
I think they've got a lunch car.

SID
(*to* AARON) Would you go get a sandwich already?

AARON
You want something?

SID
Get me a tuna.

AARON
Lou?

LOUISE
Chicken salad.

AARON
One tuna, one chicken salad.

AARON steps out.

LOUISE

Here's my problem, Sid.

SID

Oh, I know what your problem is.

LOUISE

See, I don't think you do. And that's another problem. You're
not grasping what's at stake. The power that we have, Sid.
The ability to manipulate –

SID

Manipulate?

LOUISE

What we do is going to play on eight million televisions
in the middle of an election! Not only is the opportunity
unprecedented, but so is the responsibility.

SID

It's not the first time anyone's made political ads!

LOUISE

It's the first time anyone's made them that knows how!
We can't be irresponsible on this!

SID

(*interrupting*) Your responsibility is to do what you're paid
to do! And you're better than me at doing it. So get off your
high horse and make the goddamn ads!

LOUISE

I'm not sure I want to. Not if we're going to be
careless about it.

SID

So I'm "manipulating" and I'm "careless."

LOUISE

If this is how we're going about it, then yes, it's careless.
Frankly, I've got more important things to care about.

SID

I'll tell you what I got to care about. I ain't had so much as
a raise in three years, but some hotshot female climbs up
Bernbach's ladder and now she's riding shotgun. I got that
to care about.

LOUISE

(*interrupting*) I've worked hard for everything –

SID

(*pushing through*) I got a wife and kid who need me to keep
this job. Do you got that? ... When I hear you say you've
got more important things to care about other than the one
thing it seems you do, it makes me think you got very little.

AARON returns with coffee and sandwiches.

AARON

Here we go. Coffee and sandwiches. So, listen. Tomorrow
morning, I say we start bright and early with some
brainstorming. I gotta make a schedule, I gotta book crews –

LOUISE

You got me a tuna? I asked for chicken salad.

AARON

This is all they had.

LOUISE

I hate tuna.

SID

Add it to your growing list of grievances. (*to AARON*) Did
they have any aspirin? I'm getting a headache.

AARON
(*almost unconsciously*) Come to Mama.

SID
What?

AARON
What?

SID
You getting weird on me now?

AARON
Huh?

SID
You just called yourself Mama.

AARON
Who?

LOUISE
(*recognizing*) Wait a minute.

SID
(*to AARON*) You just said "Come to Mama."

LOUISE
I know that.

AARON
Oh! Did I just say "Come to Mama"?

SID
That's what I'm telling you.

AARON
That's weird. I meant to say "Come to Bufferin."

SID
 What?

LOUISE
 It's a radio ad.

AARON
 Actually, I didn't mean to say anything. That's
 even more weird.

SID
 What?!

LOUISE
 It's for Bufferin. The aspirin. I heard it on the radio the
 other day. It's brilliant. It's three seconds. All it says is "Got a
 headache? Come to Bufferin." But the way the actor says it.
 It was soothing. Like a mother.

SID
 You mean it's an actress.

LOUISE
 No, it's a male voice. It's a man saying "Come to Bufferin,"
 but it sounds like "Come to Mama."

AARON
 I know the guy who made it. That's Tony Schwartz.

SID
 Never heard of him.

AARON
 He's a freelancer. He does these experimental things with
 sound. I've hired him a couple times.

LOUISE
 You know him?

AARON
I know everybody.

LOUISE
Can you set up a meeting?

AARON
Of course I can set up a meeting.

SID
What? No!

LOUISE
Why not?

SID
Because who says we should meet with him?

LOUISE
I do.

AARON
We could use a good sound man, Sid.

SID
If I need a sound man, I'll pick up the phone.

AARON
Sure, if all you want is a guy to point the mic.

LOUISE
(*to AARON*) This guy, Tony Schwartz. He's good?

AARON
Oh, he's good.

LOUISE
Then let's talk to him.

AARON

So let's talk to him! If we're going to go into uncharted waters, then sometimes you need to step off the boat.

LOUISE

(*after a moment*) Aaron, that doesn't make any sense.

AARON

Neither did the ketchup, and did I hassle you? You know the saying "No man is an island"? Tony will change your mind about that.

ACT I | SCENE 5

> *The basement studio of* TONY SCHWARTZ.
> *A laboratory and library of sound. At the centre is
> a desk-console, surrounded by 1964's top-of-the-line
> electronic gear. Multiple shelves contain thousands of
> boxes of reel-to-reel tape.*

> TONY *continues his lecture.*

TONY

I find it funny how my mother uses the telephone. The telephone
provides effortless, instantaneous, two-way communication. But
my mother uses it like it was a telegram: with short, functional
messages. And she yells into the phone, like she was speaking
across a canyon. (*loud*) "We'll be there Sunday at 4:30. We'll
bring potato salad." The world of communications is under the
weight of an outdated theory, which claims that if a message
sent from Point A to Point B encounters resistance, the best
solution is to repeat the message, only louder. But there is a
new theory, a far more resonant theory. ... The act of hearing
consists of momentary vibrations, which enter your ear and are
translated to your brain in a three-step process at imperceptible
speed: registering the current vibration, recalling the previous
vibrations, and anticipating future vibrations. We never hear the
continuum of sound otherwise called a word, or a sentence.
The continuum never exists at any single moment. The audience
completes the message. You will remember these words for the
rest of your ... (*waiting*) Even though I didn't say it, how many
of you heard the word "life"?

> PROJECTION: *A segment of film plays Eadweard
> Muybridge's* The Horse in Motion *(1878): a black-and-
> white, frame-by-frame sequence of a horse galloping.*

TONY

The phenomenon of motion pictures works by projecting
light onto a sequence of photographic frames at rapid speed.
Each frame is a complete image, illuminated for one-fiftieth
of a second. Following each brief moment of light is an
even briefer moment of emptiness. But it's within that dark
emptiness that our brains are illuminated.

> *PROJECTION: A series of pixels of light, like lines
> across a television, cascade down and across a screen
> at increasing speed.*

TONY

Television has brought communications into the electronic
age. With every fragment of a moment, thousands and
thousands of dots of light move across and down our screens
at unprecedented, electronic speed. But we only ever see a
single point of light at any given time.

> *On the screen, a single pixel of light remains,
> momentarily still.*

TONY

Our brain completes 99.9 percent of the picture at any
given moment. What we experience is the continuum of
registering, recalling, and anticipating, in order to give
light to that dark but never-empty space. And it's within
that deep, never-empty place that the audience completes
the message.

> *The pixel of light resumes its movement across the
> screen, increasing in number and speed, until the
> image finally takes form: the same galloping horse,
> now made up of thousands of points of light.*

TONY

The new theory is this: the audience is not a target, but
a workforce.

ACT I | SCENE 6

TONY's studio.

SOUND: Children playing in the street.

AARON, LOUISE, and SID enter.

AARON
Tony? Hey, Tony, you in here?

LOUISE
His wife said to go in.

AARON
Tony? Reenah said we could come down.

SID
Some guy, this Schwartz. Madison Avenue's top firm pays
him a visit, he's not even here. He should be coming to us.

AARON
He can't come to us.

SID
Right. He's too good for us.

AARON
No, I mean he can't. He's got a condition.

SID
What do you mean?

AARON
He's got a thing.

SID
What condition?

AARON
Forget I said it.

SID
If you don't say what he's got, then I won't work with him.

LOUISE
Sid.

SID
It could be contagious.

AARON
It's not like that. He's agoraphobic.

SID
Agoraphobic. Is that fear of heights?

AARON
Heights is acrophobia.

SID
Wait. Isn't heights vertigo?

AARON
Vertigo's with the inner ear. It's a lack of balance. Vera's got vertigo. It affects her dancing.

LOUISE
Aaron.

AARON
Agoraphobia's got to do with public places. Let's just say Tony doesn't travel well.

SID
Why should he? It's the Shangri-La in here.

LOUISE
What's wrong with this place?

SID
Nothing, if you're a hermit.

AARON
Tony's no hermit. You should see what the guy can do.
He does university lectures from here.

SID
Students come here?

AARON
No, that's just it. They're there. He's here. He does it all on
this phone gizmo.

> SID *turns off a tape player at the desk-console, which
> was the source of the children and street sounds.*

SID
Guy sounds a little weird to me.

LOUISE
What's with all the tapes?

AARON
It's his collection.

LOUISE
What's he collecting?

AARON
Everything.

SID
What do you mean?

>TONY *quietly enters the studio. Strapped around his torso is a custom-adapted tape recorder.*

AARON
>If it makes sound, he collects it. He's got this gizmo. He goes around the neighborhood recording store owners, kids, taxi drivers, zoo animals.

SID
>Why?

AARON
>For commercials, I don't know.

LOUISE
>Or maybe because no one else does. It's impressive.

SID
>So he's good at sound effects. Big deal.

TONY
>They're not sound effects.

AARON
>(*startled*) Jesus, Tony. Don't sneak up on us like that.

TONY
>How can I be sneaking? It's my studio.

>TONY *turns on his tape recorder and approaches them, holding out his microphone.*

TONY
>(*to* SID) What's your name?

SID
>Sid Myers. I'm an art director at –

TONY

You said I do sound effects. I have no interest in sound
effects. I'm more interested in the effect of sound on people.

SID

(*after a moment*) Alright.

TONY

(*to AARON*) Did you see Reenah?

AARON

Yeah, she told us to come down.

TONY

(*to LOUISE*) Reenah's my wife.

LOUISE

She's lovely.

> *TONY approaches her, microphone out.*

TONY

I think so, too. What's your name?

SID

What is this? An interview?

TONY

It's only an interview if you say something interesting.
(*to LOUISE*) What's your name?

LOUISE

Lou. Louise. Whichever you prefer.

TONY

(*tests them out*) Lou. Louise. Louise ends on an upwards
inflection, which is a more pleasant sound. You said you
found my collection impressive. You should listen to it

sometime. (*to the group*) Aaron tells me you need my help on the Johnson campaign.

AARON
That's not exactly how I put it, Tony.

TONY
But it's the case nevertheless. If I know anything about Madison Avenue, it's that you absolutely need my help.

SID
Is he yanking my chain? Who's this guy think he is?

TONY
I'm the guy whose ideas are going to be talked about fifty years from now. (*to SID*) How would you define your assignment?

SID
My assignment?

TONY
Yes. How would you define it?

SID
I'm the guy who's going to help Lyndon Johnson beat Rockefeller. That's who I am.

TONY
You see, that's why you need me. You don't know your assignment.

> *Darkness. Then, as the scene transitions,*
> *we hear the dulcet male voice of a radio commercial*
> *ANNOUNCER.*

ANNOUNCER
Got a headache? Come to Bufferin.

ACT I | SCENE 7

PROJECTION (text): May 1964
The work room at Doyle Dane Bernbach.

*LOUISE and SID are leafing through binders, each
one filled with newspaper and magazine articles and
other documents.*

SID
   I'm telling you, the research Clifford sent over, it's
   impressive. You finding stuff?

LOUISE
   Uh-huh.

SID
   This is ammunition.

LOUISE
   I think my eyes have gunpowder burns.

SID
   And we haven't even looked at what Clifford's got
   on Goldwater.

LOUISE
   I'm telling you, it'll be Rockefeller.

SID
   Goldwater's doing better than expected, Lou. The Nebraska
   primary, Indiana, Texas, Illinois.

LOUISE
   And come California, he's finished.

SID

From what I'm seeing here, Rockefeller hasn't got much to worry about. Wealthy businessman. Progressive moderate. Successful governor.

LOUISE

(*reading from her binder*) "Proven adulterer."

SID

Hey, now.

LOUISE

"Wife-stealer."

SID

Sounds like you got the better binder.

LOUISE

Poll after poll, public opinion on Rockefeller's divorce and new wife. And not the highest of opinions. (*closing the binder*) So much for elevating the discourse ... I'd like to hear what Tony's got in mind.

SID

Schwartz? What does he know?

LOUISE

I've been listening to his ads. There's something about his work. He's different.

SID

He's different, alright.

AARON enters, loaded with binders.

AARON

Here's the file on Goldwater.

LOUISE
  File? That's a library!

SID
  Like I said. Clifford delivered. I'm impressed.

AARON
  Takes more than a few binders to impress me. White House
  Deputy Special Counsel. He doesn't even get his own ashtray.
  (*reading from magazine article*) Check out this quote I found
  on Goldwater: "Sometimes I think this country would be better
  if we could just saw off the Eastern Seaboard."

SID
  What a swell guy.

AARON
  It's from an exposé in *Good Housekeeping*.

LOUISE
  The White House keeps tabs on *Good Housekeeping*?

AARON
  It's an interview with Mrs. Goldwater. Listen to this.

LOUISE
  Hold on a second! The man's wife?

SID
  She did the interview.

AARON
  (*referring to same article*) In answering a question about
  the Senator's health, Mrs. Goldwater said, quote, "on two
  occasions, my husband's nerves broke completely."

LOUISE
  (*grabbing the article*) Let me see that.

SID

A potential Republican nominee had two nervous breakdowns. That's ammunition right there.

LOUISE

Thirty years ago!

SID

A breakdown's a breakdown.

LOUISE

You're giving me a breakdown.

AARON

(*from a news article*) A reporter asks Goldwater about the White House plan to put a man on the moon. His answer? "I don't want to hit the moon. I want to lob one into the men's room of the Kremlin."

LOUISE

Lob what?

AARON

What do you think?! A nuclear bomb!

LOUISE

It's hyperbole. Goldwater's an Arizona cowboy. He's not seriously advocating –

SID

Lou, the guy's not level-headed.

LOUISE

And you two are a couple of vultures.

SID

And you need to put away the white gloves!

LOUISE

This is what I'm talking about. These are presidential nominees.
We're not going into their bedrooms. We're not going after
their wives. And we're not going to turn our opponent into the
boogeyman. Show me something that matters!

SID

(*from another news article*) "When asked how he would
characterize the nation's nuclear arsenal, Senator Goldwater
referred to the bomb as 'merely another weapon.'"

AARON

Aw, geez.

SID

Goldwater is then asked, if he was President, how he
would deal with enemy supply routes in Vietnam, to which
Goldwater says low-yield nuclear weapons are something
that could be considered.

AARON

Who's he kidding, "low yield"?

SID

(*to LOUISE*) How's that for "not advocating"?

AARON

Go shoot yourself with a low-yield bullet.

> SID *pulls out a newspaper article, holds it up for*
> *all to see.*

SID

Yesterday's headline in the *San Francisco Examiner*:
"Goldwater's Plan to Use Vietnam A-Bomb. 'I'd Risk a War.'"

AARON

All the Way with LBJ.

ACT I | SCENE 8

CLIFFORD's basement office at the White House.

CLIFFORD listens to PRESIDENT JOHNSON delivering a speech on the radio.

PRESIDENT
(*on radio*) Your imagination, your initiative, and your indignation will determine whether we build a society where progress is the servant of our needs, or a society where old values and new visions are buried under unbridled growth.

CLIFFORD
Yes.

PRESIDENT
For in your time we have the opportunity to move not only toward the rich society and the powerful society, but upward to the Great Society.

CLIFFORD
Come on now. We need to hear it.

PRESIDENT
The Great Society rests on abundance and liberty for all. It demands an end to poverty and racial injustice, to which we are totally committed in our time.

Applause from the radio. CLIFFORD turns it off.

CLIFFORD
We're on our way. We are on our way.

CLIFFORD picks up the phone and dials the switchboard.

CLIFFORD
(*on phone*) Geraldine, it's Clifford Lewis. (*listening*) Lewis.
(*listening*) From the basement, yes. Could you take down a
message for the President, please? ... Mr. President, I want
you to know that what you've put forward with the Great
Society ... As a citizen, I'm forever grateful. But as your
adviser, there will be a cost. It's a treacherous road ahead, sir,
but if you are the man to deliver justice in our time ... then I
will stand by you on that road ... Thank you, Geraldine.

> CLIFFORD *hangs up. He sings from the hymn*
> *"We'll Understand it Better By and By" (1903)*
> *by Charles Albert Tindley.*

By and by, when the morning comes,
When the saints of God are gathering home,
We'll tell the story of how we've overcome,
For we'll understand it better by and by.

ACT I | SCENE 9

PROJECTION (*text*): June 1964

A hallway outside the work room
at Doyle Dane Bernbach.

SID and LOUISE are in mid-conversation.

SID

I don't know why Mr. Bernbach asked you to do the pitch.
I do plenty of pitches. Why don't we both do it?

LOUISE

Because he asked me.

SID

I don't even know if you're on board with it.

LOUISE

I'm on board.

SID

You better be, because Mr. Bernbach is definitely on board.

BERNBACH enters.

BERNBACH

Sidney. Louise. Shouldn't you be getting ready?

SID

We're just going over the final details.

BERNBACH

Is Clifford here?

SID

He's inside with Aaron.

BERNBACH
Clifford's in the room?

SID
Yeah.

BERNBACH
With Aaron?

SID
Yeah.

BERNBACH
(*to* SID) Then I suggest you get in there.

SID
Yeah.

    SID exits.

BERNBACH
Don't be nervous.

LOUISE
I'm fine.

BERNBACH
It's alright to be nervous. We're carrying a lot more
risk than usual.

LOUISE
How do you mean?

BERNBACH
Our Republican clients aren't pleased. We lost two accounts
today alone.

LOUISE
You must've expected that.

BERNBACH
True. I didn't expect to lose Bob Thompson.

LOUISE
Bob Thompson? He's Head Copywriter.

BERNBACH
And a committed Republican, who has taken his services to the competition … Impress me, Louise.

BERNBACH exits.

The scene shifts to inside the work room. LOUISE enters, with CLIFFORD, BERNBACH, SID, and AARON already present. AARON is trying to get a film projector to work.

CLIFFORD
Nice to see you again, Miss Brown. I'm excited for what you have to show.

SID
If we can ever get around to starting.

AARON
For Pete's sake, I don't know why I can't get it to work. It was fine an hour ago.

BERNBACH
Then it should be fine now.

AARON
Where are the damn instructions?

TONY enters.

SID
Look who showed up.

TONY
No one told me we were meeting on such a high floor.

AARON
You'll be fine, Tony.

TONY
It's the 14th floor.

SID
Just take a seat, would ya?

TONY
I'll stand near the door.

> TONY *removes his shoes and socks (a coping mechanism for his agoraphobia).*

CLIFFORD
Who's this?

LOUISE
This is Tony Schwartz. He's working with us.

CLIFFORD
I didn't approve any other –

AARON
I can vouch for Tony. He's a total pro.

> *They all look over and see* TONY, *now barefoot, holding his shoes.*

TONY
Pardon me.

CLIFFORD
I'm not referring to his qualifications.

BERNBACH
    He's a Democrat.

TONY
    What?

AARON
    You have to be a Democrat.

TONY
    Forever?

AARON
    Tony –

TONY
    Do I have to sign in blood?

SID
    Hey, Schwartz –

TONY
    Why would I be here if I wasn't a Democrat?

BERNBACH
    May we begin? If Aaron can get the projector to work.

AARON
    I'm trying, Mr. Bernbach. I can't seem to ...

        TONY *moves to the projector, hands his shoes to*
        AARON. *He makes an adjustment, then flips the*
        switch. The reels start turning. TONY *retrieves his*
        shoes, then turns to BERNBACH.

TONY
    You're Bill Bernbach.

BERNBACH
I am. Thank you for fixing the projector.

TONY
It's just an old model.

BERNBACH
Some say the same of me.

TONY
No one does. That's false modesty. Any chance we can do this on a lower floor?

SID
The film's starting. Would you sit down?

    PROJECTION: A commercial from the 1952
    presidential election, in which a WOMAN talks to
    PRESIDENT EISENHOWER:

ANNOUNCER
(*recorded*) Eisenhower answers America.

WOMAN
(*on screen*) The Democrats have made mistakes, but aren't their intentions good?

EISENHOWER
(*on screen*) Well, if the driver of your school bus runs into a truck, hits a lamppost, drives into a ditch, you don't say his intentions are good. You get a new bus driver.

    AARON turns off the projector.
    LOUISE takes the floor.

LOUISE
In 1952, Dwight Eisenhower won a decisive victory to become president through a campaign that owed much of

its success to television. Eisenhower was smart enough to know that he didn't know anything about television, so he trusted an ad agency to deliver an innovative campaign, including these short, twenty-second spot ads. But what was innovative then is horribly out of date now.

TONY

Speaking of short, how long's this meeting?

AARON

Tony.

LOUISE

Whether it was Eisenhower in '52, Eisenhower again in '56, or Kennedy four years ago, the candidate who understood television became president. What we've come up with is a strategy for the most effective use of television ever in a political campaign.

> *LOUISE moves to an easel, with several boards on it. She turns the first board. It says: "Theatrical images over speechmaking."*

LOUISE

Theatrical images over speechmaking. Politicians shouldn't use campaign ads to make speeches.

CLIFFORD

The President likes to make speeches.

LOUISE

And there's nothing wrong with speeches –

SID

But they make for bad television. Images have far more impact.

LOUISE

(*resuming control*) Which bring us to:

> *LOUISE flips to the next board: "The commercials do not show the President."*

LOUISE

The commercials do not show the President. The thinking here is that –

CLIFFORD

Are you serious?

LOUISE

Yes.

CLIFFORD

The commercials don't show the President. The commercials that are meant to get him elected.

LOUISE

That's correct.

CLIFFORD

(*to BERNBACH*) Have you approved these?

BERNBACH

I have.

CLIFFORD

Tell me why, in the middle of a presidential campaign, we're not including the President in his own commercials?

TONY

For one thing, he's not very good-looking.

CLIFFORD

What was that?

AARON
Not now, Tony.

TONY
I suggest we don't use his voice either.

CLIFFORD
Who are you?

> *Clutching his shoes,* TONY *paces out the perimeter*
> *of the room.*

TONY
I'm Tony Schwartz. I'm not sure if I have a title. You could
call me a media theorist, or a researcher. You could call me
an ad man like these folks, but that's like taking a kitten and
a lion and calling them both cats.

BERNBACH
I beg your pardon?

SID
We're in the middle of a presentation.

TONY
With concepts I came up with.

SID
That's bull.

TONY
I'd elaborate but I'm not really comfortable this far from my
house. Or this high up. Now, as for the President. The way I see it,
he poses several challenges. The first is he's just not good-looking.

SID
Now, hold on –

TONY

The man's not telegenic, which has a negative impact on voters. Which brings me to the President's voice. It has a sound that makes me, how do I say this, recoil.

AARON

Tony!

BERNBACH

Whose presentation is this?

TONY

The next challenge is that when people do see Johnson they can't help but think of Kennedy, which brings up such terrible sadness.

SID

I can barely put up with this.

TONY

Neither can I. There's no air circulation. Your next challenge is that no matter how skilled a politician Johnson is, that's how people perceive him. A skilled politician. You might as well be a skilled pickpocket.

SID

That's it! He just called the President a pickpocket.

LOUISE

He's calling him a politician, Sid. You can't tell me Johnson doesn't have a reputation for being slick.

BERNBACH

Louise!

TONY

I'm not questioning his character. He had my vote with the Great Society. And if he passes Civil Rights I'll lead the parade. Well, for about eight blocks. After that I get uncomfortable.

BERNBACH
(*to LOUISE, forceful*) Would you please continue?

LOUISE
Now this next one is definitely a new direction for us. But it's
something that ...

   She hesitates.

SID
Come on, Lou.

   *LOUISE flips to the next board: "Unrelentingly
   combative."*

LOUISE
Unrelentingly combative ... Right from the start, we're going
to ... we're going to attack our opponent, regardless of ...
Do you hear how that sounds, Mr. Bernbach?

SID
Lou –

BERNBACH
This isn't the time for –

LOUISE
No matter who the Republicans nominate –

CLIFFORD
What's going on?

LOUISE
– we're just going to attack?

SID
(*to CLIFFORD*) Nothing's going on –

LOUISE

(*to BERNBACH*) You told me this firm was built on
principles. You told me you wouldn't allow that to change –

BERNBACH

That's enough, Louise!

Pause.

TONY

Maybe while you figure this out I can leave. Another few
minutes, you'll have to scrape me out of a closet.

BERNBACH

Fine.

TONY starts to head out.

BERNBACH

Now, Clifford, in terms of the President's policy
achievements, which areas do –

TONY

Did you say "policy achievements"?

AARON

Tony, you should go.

TONY

Does anyone here have a degree in psychology? I know
you're all masters of human nature, but has anyone here
studied psychology?

SID

And you have?

TONY

Not formally, but I am seeing a therapist. You're ignoring a crucial element, which is the psychology of how people vote. People think two candidates equals two options. But there're four options. You can vote for or against either candidate. Psychologically, that's huge. Johnson's policy achievements don't matter, because this election isn't about Johnson.

CLIFFORD

Johnson's achievements are some of the most –

TONY

(*to* CLIFFORD) Do you want to talk about policy or do you want to win?

BERNBACH

(*cold*) Thank you, Tony.

TONY

You're welcome, Bill.

AARON

(*to* TONY) Let me take you down to the lobby.

BERNBACH

Louise will escort Mr. Schwartz. And may I suggest she take an early lunch.

LOUISE and TONY exit.

ACT I | SCENE 10

> *TONY's studio, shortly after.*
>
> *TONY is systematically opening up the electronic floodgates, turning on each tape player, radio, and television at his disposal, finding comfort in cacophony.*
>
> *LOUISE enters behind him, hovering at the door.*
>
> *The first and loudest SOUND is that of a children's clap-and-rhythm game.*

CHILDREN
 (*recorded*) 1, 2, 3 and a zing zing zing
 Number 1.
 Who, me?
 Yes, you.
 Not me.
 Then who?

LOUISE
 (*shouting*) Tony, are you –

CHILDREN
 Jack-O-Lin
 Who, me?
 Yes, you.
 Couldn't be.
 Then who?

LOUISE
 (*shouting*) Should I just leave?

CHILDREN
 Number 2.

Who, me?
Yes, you.
Couldn't be.
Then, who?

LOUISE
(*shouting*) Could you turn some of these down?

TONY
(*shouting*) What?

LOUISE
(*shouting*) The sound! Could you turn some of it down?

> TONY *shuts down various machines but leaves*
> *one track playing: the sound of a puppy barking,*
> *as piercing as it is sudden.*

LOUISE
(*startled*) What the hell is that?

TONY
It's a dog.

LOUISE
I know it's a dog, but what –

NARRATOR
(*on tape*) It was little more than a year ago that a puppy was brought to the shelter for homeless animals on New York's Upper East Side. At the same time, there was a young man named Tony Schwartz …

LOUISE
What is this?

NARRATOR
(*continuing*) ... who lived alone in an apartment on the West
Side of town. And Tony decided ...

TONY *lowers the volume.*

NARRATOR
(*continuing, low volume*) ... that what he wanted most in life
at this moment was a dog ...

TONY
(*speaking over*) I made this with my partner Elliott. I was
living on my own. I thought I should get a dog. Elliott said
we should document the experience.

NARRATOR
(*continuing, low volume*) ... It was February 3, 1956,
when Tony Schwartz appeared at the information desk
at the animal shelter to ask for a dog. An ordinary, plain,
everyday dog.

ATTENDANT
(*continuing, low volume*) You have to sign an
application here ...

LOUISE
(*speaking over*) I didn't know you had a partner.
Who's Elliott?

TONY *turns off the tape player.*

TONY
We're not partners anymore ... Let me pay you back
for the cab.

LOUISE
Forget it. Let the company pay.

TONY
Thanks for getting me home. It's not like I needed –

LOUISE
We were both a little frazzled.

TONY
Are you alright?

LOUISE
Sure. It's nothing a room full of noise can't cure.

TONY
You thought that was noise?

LOUISE
No, I meant –

TONY
They say noise is in the ear of the beholder.

LOUISE
Cute ... Well, I should –

TONY
Are you hungry? I could get Reenah to make some sandwiches. She makes great tuna salad –

LOUISE
No, I'm fine.

TONY
It'd be nice if you stick around.

LOUISE
(*after a moment*) Alright.

TONY

I hope I wasn't too embarrassing at the meeting.

LOUISE

Why? Because you had to leave?

TONY

I left because I had to. I mean I hope I didn't embarrass
anyone with my comments.

LOUISE

I'd say my outburst provided more than enough cover.

TONY

You challenged your boss in front of the client. Took a jab at
the President.

LOUISE

I'm just figuring things out.

TONY

Like the shoe salesman who thinks we should all
go barefoot.

LOUISE

I'm not rejecting what we do.

TONY

Are you sure?

LOUISE

(*cautious*) So what was that? With you. During the pitch.
Was that your agoraphobia? Are there situations you
can't handle?

TONY

It wasn't the situation. It was the location. I tend to stay
within a certain area.

LOUISE
How big's the area?

TONY
About eight blocks, north to south; four, east to west.

LOUISE
That's not big.

She moves to the shelves.

LOUISE
What's on all these tapes? The world of sound?

TONY
More or less.

LOUISE
That's some hobby.

TONY
Hobby? That's going to be in a museum someday.

LOUISE
You've got a healthy opinion of yourself.

TONY
Someone should.

LOUISE
You use these tapes in your commercials?

TONY
Sometimes. If it's the right sound, sure.

LOUISE
If it's not a hobby, if it's not work, what's it for?

TONY

(*after a moment*) When I was sixteen I went blind. My sight came back, obviously. It was only a few months. It was the agoraphobia that brought it on. And what happened was, although I couldn't see, the world of sound just opened up ... I might not be able to travel to France, or Japan, or Philadelphia, even. But the world comes to me. Just about every kind of music, every kind of human interaction, is on one of these tapes ... Can I play you something?

LOUISE

Does it involve dogs?

TONY

Recently I've become fascinated with numbers. I've got about twelve hours on tape, all different uses of numbers.

LOUISE

Only twelve?

TONY

You can either be dismissive like your colleagues, or you can admit you're curious.

> *TONY loads the tape.*

TONY

Numbers have great symbolic value, especially if you juxtapose the meanings. Imagine a secretary listening as the clock counts down the last ten seconds at work. Now imagine a mother listening to the same clock count down her son's final seconds in the electric chair.

> *He starts the machine, then grabs a set of headphones.*
>
> *SOUND: A radio commercial plays.*

ANNOUNCER
(*recorded*) Sometimes, numbers can be fun.

BOY
(*recorded, faltering, playful*) 1, 2, 3, 4, 5, 6, 8, 9, 12, 14, 16, 18, 10.

MALE COUNTDOWN VOICE
(*recorded, authoritative*) 10 ... 9 ... 8 ...

TONY
Now. Listen.

> *TONY places the headphones over LOUISE's ears, and plugs them in.*

> *LOUISE continues listening. What she hears is unnerving. She abruptly removes the headphones and pulls out the cord.*

> *The ending plays on the loudspeakers: an atomic explosion.*

ANNOUNCER
Sometimes.

> *TONY stops the tape.*

LOUISE
What was that?

TONY
It's an anti-nuclear spot I made for the United Nations. You see what I mean, about numbers? I took the young child counting to ten, and then I juxtaposed it with the launch –

LOUISE
No, I get it. I definitely get it. God, it's like I just watched an atomic bomb drop on a room full of kids.

TONY

That's what it made you do. Actually, that's what you
made yourself do. It's a theory I'm working on. Electronic
messages designed to bring to the surface what's already
deep inside. It's about hearing what's already there ...
Do you like it?

LOUISE

Like it? It's terrifying.

TONY

Frightening people is one way of motivating them.

LOUISE

Motivate them to do what? ... You're not suggesting we use
this in the campaign?

TONY

It sounds like we could use a big idea.

LOUISE

For one thing, how would that play against Rockefeller? If it
was Goldwater, maybe, but that's not happening.

TONY

And if it does?

LOUISE

Bernbach likes things subtle, Tony. That's about as subtle as
a sledgehammer.

TONY

And a lot more effective.

LOUISE

(impressed) You're a lot more than a sound effects
guy, aren't you.

ACT I | SCENE 11

The work room at Doyle Dane Bernbach. Late in the evening.

SID is dressed casually and drinking beer from a six-pack. AARON has a little black book, and is making calls.

Written on a chalkboard:
   "Goldwater Spots: i) Social Security,
   ii) Eastern Seaboard, iii) Merely Another Weapon
   Rockefeller Spots: i) Mr. Establishment,
   ii) Silver Spoon, iii) Divorce"

SID

So, I'm over at the library. I'm on the steps eating a hot dog. It's gorgeous out. There's two girls sitting nearby. Secretaries. They're having a smoke. A black girl and a white girl.

AARON

(*on the phone*) Yeah, hi, I'd like to leave a message for Drummond Drury. Tell him it's Aaron Ehrlich. Tell him to give me a call first thing Monday. Or Sunday, if possible. Or tonight, if he can.

He hangs up.

SID

So get this. Each girl, at the same time, butts out her cigarette on the steps.

AARON

Drummond's still with the Unger Agency, right?

SID

He's a cameraman. How should I know? (*continuing story*)
So this police officer walks by. He barks, and I mean barks at
the black girl. "What do you think you're doing, desecrating
public property?" Over a cigarette. But both girls did it.

AARON

(*flipping through his book*) Who else should I call?

SID

It's nine o'clock Saturday night. Have a beer!

AARON

How can you be so cavalier? It's not like Mr. Bernbach to call
us in like this. Something's up.

SID

Yeah, your blood pressure.

AARON

He sounded upset on the phone. I want to be prepared.

SID

Now, the cop, he's laying into the black girl. He starts writing
a ticket. So I step in.

AARON

You stepped in?

SID

"Officer," I say, "I can't help but notice you singled out
only one of these two women, when it appears they each
committed the same infraction."

AARON

You didn't.

SID

Like I was Atticus Finch!

LOUISE enters, dressed for a night out.
She has a newspaper.

SID

Look at this! Mr. Bernbach interrupted date night, huh,
kiddo? Tough break. (*continuing story*) So the cop comes up
to me. "And who the hell are you?" "I'm Sid Myers. I'm the
guy who's going to help elect the president who just signed
the Civil Rights Act."

LOUISE

We're having beers, are we?

SID

It's Saturday night. Who's the lucky fellow?

LOUISE

Not that it's any of your business, but I was out with
a girlfriend.

SID

No wonder you're single. (*continuing story*) So now there's
a crowd. The girls are smiling. The cop puffs out his chest.
"Well, I didn't vote for Johnson." So I say, "Nobody did, but
they sure as hell will in November."

LOUISE

Where's Mr. Bernbach?

AARON

On his way down. Whatever this is about, this time I know
it's not good.

LOUISE

> Not so soon, my bespectacled friend. I think everything's
> about to line up exactly the way it should.

SID

> What do you mean?

> *LOUISE plops down the newspaper and grabs a beer.*

LOUISE

> Check today's poll. Three days before the California primary,
> Rockefeller's up fifteen points. Goldwater's finished.

> *As SID and AARON look at the newspaper, LOUISE*
> *goes to the chalkboard. She chalks out a circle around*
> *the section on Rockefeller.*

LOUISE

> Bernbach's coming to tell us the good news. It's Johnson
> versus Rockefeller. Policy against policy. This is what
> elections are about. Not all this Goldwater crap.

> *BERNBACH and CLIFFORD enter.*

SID

> Mr. Bernbach. How are you doing tonight?

AARON

> You didn't say Clifford was coming in. Did I do
> something wrong?

> *BERNBACH goes to the case of beer.*

BERNBACH

> I wasn't aware I'd convened a social gathering.

SID

> Well, it's Saturday night.

LOUISE
  I'd say we've got reason to celebrate. We're getting our
  marching orders, aren't we? Have a drink with us.

BERNBACH
  Is this a saloon, Louise?

LOUISE
  (*after a moment*) No, sir.

BERNBACH
  Before he got on the train, Clifford telephoned to relay
  the President's frustration – (*then angrily*) the *President's*
  frustration – with our lack of progress!

SID
  We're all working hard, Mr. Bernbach.

CLIFFORD
  Not from what I'm seeing.

AARON
  I'm sorry?

CLIFFORD
  You're weeks behind schedule.

SID
  Clifford, I know you're under pressure. The White House
  wants to see some ads. It's not like we're twiddling our
  thumbs. We've got all kinds of ideas.

CLIFFORD
  You mean what's up on the board? I've seen the scripts for
  all of these.

        CLIFFORD goes to the board, and grabs a
        piece of chalk.

CLIFFORD
Trying to get folks worried about their retirement.

He draws a line through "Social Security."

AARON
What the heck?

CLIFFORD
A half-assed spot that's nothing more than a gimmick.

He draws a line through "Eastern Seaboard."

AARON
Get a load of this guy.

AARON puts his feet up onto a desk.

CLIFFORD
And on the nuclear issue, nothing more than a sarcastic joke.

He draws a line through "Merely Another Weapon."

CLIFFORD
I asked for urgency. I asked for a weapon. You've
given me nothing.

AARON
Someone's position's gone to his head.

CLIFFORD
What did you say?

SID
These are all good spots, Clifford. We're giving you what –

CLIFFORD
(*to AARON*) Would you mind taking your feet off the desk?

AARON
Is this your desk?

CLIFFORD
When I'm speaking, take your feet off the desk.

AARON
Don't go punching above your weight, pal.

BERNBACH
Aaron!

AARON *complies.*

CLIFFORD
Do I need to remind you what's at stake? Do I need to remind you that we're trying to avoid nuclear war? You want to talk boxing? I asked for a knockout punch. You haven't stepped inside the ring!

LOUISE
Because we're wasting our time on two candidates! Rockefeller's up fifteen points. Let's stop wasting time on Barry Goldwater! It's Rockefeller we should be discussing.

CLIFFORD
Rockefeller pulled out of the race.

CLIFFORD *goes to the board.*

LOUISE
What?

CLIFFORD *pulls Rockefeller's photo off the board, erases the Rockefeller ideas.*

LOUISE
What are you doing? The California primary's in three days
and Rockefeller's up fifteen points!

BERNBACH
And his wife just gave birth this morning.

SID
What?

AARON
You mean ...?

BERNBACH
Rockefeller's wife of eight months just delivered their baby.

LOUISE
No ...

CLIFFORD
We heard from Rockefeller's campaign manager this
afternoon. He'll concede tomorrow.

AARON
You mean that ... Barry Goldwater ...

BERNBACH
He may have been a fool in April, but he's the
nominee in June.

SID
What do you need us to do?

CLIFFORD
We need to destroy Barry Goldwater. The stakes are too
high not to.

BERNBACH
There's your marching orders.

CLIFFORD and BERNBACH leave.

AARON
I need to call people. There's people I need to call.

LOUISE
This can't be.

SID
It is.

LOUISE
It can't. He can't run for president.

AARON
He won't win. He can't win. We're not gonna let him.

SID
That's right.

AARON
We're going to stop him. How we gonna do that?

SID goes to the board and the remaining
Goldwater material.

SID
We got three good Goldwater ads. These are good ads!
I don't know why Cliff doesn't –

LOUISE
Because they're not strong enough. They're not
hard enough.

SID

We go after Goldwater for being a cowboy. For being a radical. We go after all the stupid things he says.

LOUISE

Clifford's right. We haven't even stepped in the ring.

AARON

Go after the fact that any shrink in the country would have Goldwater certified before you counted to three. Go after the fact that he's a Grade A moron!

LOUISE

(*an idea springs*) Wait a second ...

SID

What? We make an ad that says "Barry Goldwater's a moron"?

AARON

Is he or is he not?!

LOUISE

(*to herself*) Before you counted to three ... That's it! I've got it. (*launching*) Aaron, what are you afraid of?

AARON

Everything!

LOUISE

No. What are we all afraid of? What do we fear?

SID

(*after a moment*) The atom bomb.

LOUISE

Aaron, when I point to you, I want you to count up from one to ten.

AARON
Okay.

LOUISE
(*to AARON*) The sweetest, littlest voice you've got. (*to SID*)
Sid, when I point to you, count down. Deep. Dark.

LOUISE makes a pitch.

LOUISE
It's a beautiful day. The sun's shining. It's quiet. It's peaceful.
There's a boy ... No. It's a girl. She's counting. She's counting
petals off a flower.

She cues AARON.

AARON
1, 2 ...

LOUISE
Higher!

AARON
(*higher pitch, like a kid*) ... 3, 4, 5 ...

LOUISE
(*speaking over*) An innocent girl. Five, six years
old. Not afraid.

AARON
... 6, 7, 8, 9, 10.

She cues SID. He launches into a countdown.

SID
10 ... 9 ... 8 ...

LOUISE
  She's looks up. She's frightened.

SID
  ... 7 ... 6 ... 5 ... 4 ...

LOUISE
  She thought she was safe. She's not safe.

SID
  ... 3 ... 2 ... 1 –

LOUISE
  And then all we hear is ...

> *LOUISE acts out the sound of an atomic explosion.*
> *She lets the dust settle.*

LOUISE
  Vote for President Johnson on November 3rd.

SID
  (*after a moment*) Where did you come up with that?

> *She doesn't say.*

> *Lights out.*

> *End of Act One.*

ACT II

ACT II | SCENE 1

PROJECTION (text): July 16, 1964
SOUND: A crowd, growing in frenzy.

VOICES
  Barry! Barry! Barry!

TONY's studio. Late at night.

*With tensions and temperatures high, electric fans
spin in vain, and a creative team spins its wheels.
A television plays coverage of the Republican
convention, muted.*

*LOUISE inspects campaign posters tacked up on
a board. Johnson's "All the Way With LBJ," and
Goldwater's "In Your Heart You Know He's Right."*

SID tests out a script, with AARON on a stopwatch.

SID
  Not long ago, people tested atomic bombs in the
  atmosphere. Radioactive fallout filled with strontium-90 and
  cesium-137 fell from the sky into children's ice cream. What
  did we do? We signed the Nuclear Test-Ban Treaty. Barry
  Goldwater voted against this treaty.

AARON
  (*quick with the tag line*) Vote for President Johnson on
  November 3rd.

SID
  How long?

AARON
  Twenty-two seconds.

SID

Lou, can you cut two seconds off "Ice Cream"?

LOUISE

Can you deliver it less like you're in a horror movie?

SID

It's the voice of intimidation.

LOUISE

It's not working.

SID

You wrote it.

TONY enters with a tray of sandwiches.

LOUISE

Then I'm allowed to say it's not working. Tony.

TONY

What?

LOUISE

We're testing "Ice Cream." Did you read it?

TONY

I did.

LOUISE

Any thoughts?

TONY

Who do you want it to resonate with?

SID

Voters.

LOUISE
(*regarding her sandwich*) Tuna?

TONY
If it's about poisoned ice cream, who is it that typically buys ice cream?

AARON
Mothers.

TONY
Get an actress to do the voice. Better yet, get an actress who's a mother. Better still, get a mother who's not an actress. The day after it plays you'll have 50,000 mothers in the grocery store terrified about Barry Goldwater.

LOUISE
Aaron.

AARON
(*writing a note in his book*) Find a mother.

SID
(*pointing to the television*) Hey, look. There's Rockefeller. Tony, turn it up. I want to hear his speech.

AARON
You mean his concession speech.

> *TONY turns up the volume.*

> PROJECTION: *Television footage of Nelson Rockefeller at the Republican National Convention.*

AARON
There he is. Poor ol' Rocky. The nomination should've been his.

SID
  Can you believe the dumb luck? Three days before the
  California primary, the new wife pops out a scandal.

LOUISE
  I still can't believe it's Goldwater.

ROCKEFELLER
  (*on screen*) During this year, I have criss-crossed this
  nation fighting for these principles, fighting to keep the
  Republican Party ...

          The television crowd jeers.

LOUISE
  What's that? Are they booing him?

ROCKEFELLER
  ... fighting to keep the Republican Party the party of
  all the people.

          The crowd applauds.

AARON
  There you go, Rocky.

ROCKEFELLER
  And warning of the extremist threat, its danger to
  the Party ...

SID
  He just accused his own party of being extremist.

LOUISE
  Can you blame him?

          ROCKEFELLER is drowned out by the mob.

AARON

The crowd won't let him speak. They're heckling him.

LOUISE

Have you ever seen anything like this? At a national convention?

TONY

Listen.

The crowd chants "We want Barry!"

AARON

"We want Barry."

SID

I heard two black reporters were chased out of the convention by Goldwater's mob. I hear he's got supporters in the Ku Klux Klan. (*pointing to Goldwater poster*) "In your heart, you know he's right." How about "In your head, you know he might." With a mushroom cloud.

AARON

Hey, that's good.

SID

"In your guts, you know he's nuts!"

AARON

Watch out, Lou. You got competition!

SID

I'm just getting started. You know what this is? It's a crusade. I'm a crusader. Barry Goldwater and the Republicans won't know what hit 'em.

TONY surreptitiously plays a tape.

SOUND: Wagner's "Ride of the Valkyries" (1870).

SID

(*continuing, oblivious*) I'm coming after you, Barry, like a dog in a meat market. 'Cause that's what we should be doing! Maybe it's time all this ethics and civility – (*finally hearing the music*) What the hell is that?

TONY

It's crusade music.

SID

(*turning off the tape*) Can we be serious?!

LOUISE

Look. Here comes Goldwater.

> *As the televised convention footage continues,*
> *BARRY GOLDWATER is on the platform,*
> *basking in applause.*

> *TONY sets up a microphone to record it.*

AARON

There he is. Mr. Conservative. What's Goldwater got to say about thugs in his own party?

LOUISE

Just you watch. They rant and rave during the primaries, then they soften the edges. It's always the way. He'll cool down the rhetoric.

SID

Ten bucks says he won't.

LOUISE

Fine. It's not my mortgage.

> *BARRY GOLDWATER is in the midst of his*
> *acceptance speech.*

GOLDWATER
(*on screen*) Let our Republicanism so focused and so
dedicated not be made fuzzy and feudal by unthinking and
stupid labels.

SID
Who you calling stupid, Barry? The Klan in your own party.

Goldwater utters the famous quote:

GOLDWATER
I would remind you that extremism in the defense of
liberty is no vice.

The crowd erupts in applause.

LOUISE
What did he just say?

AARON
Did he just promote extremism?

SID
Look. Richard Nixon can't believe it.

LOUISE
Someone write it down. What did he say?

TONY
"Extremism in the defense of liberty is no vice."

LOUISE
He's calling for extremism.

AARON
I hope Vera's not watching this.

SID
Listen to the crowd. They love it.

LOUISE
Here. He's coming back now.

GOLDWATER
And let me remind you also that moderation in the pursuit of justice is no virtue.

More applause.

AARON
Aw, geez.

LOUISE
My God.

TONY
Moderation in the pursuit of justice is not a virtue.

AARON
Since when's moderation not a virtue?

SID
So much for softening the edges. It looks like Goldwater's going to run as Goldwater. (*pointing to the screen*) Look at this. Insanity gets a standing ovation.

LOUISE
This is horrible. Turn it off.

TONY turns off the television.

AARON
That was terrifying.

LOUISE
That man can't run for President. That's not the
Republican Party.

SID
It is now. The whole country just moved six inches
to the right.

LOUISE
That's not the Republican Party! At least not the Party
I grew up with.

Pause.

SID
What was that?

LOUISE
(*steeling herself*) I grew up in a Republican house.

AARON
Do you mean, like, your family owned one of those
heritage homes?

LOUISE
My father's a Republican. His father was. My
family's Republican. The first time I voted was
for Eisenhower in 1952.

SID
Lou.

LOUISE
I voted for him again in '56.

AARON
Heck, everyone voted for Eisenhower in '56.

LOUISE
I voted for Richard Nixon over Jack Kennedy.

SID
(*after a moment*) You lied to us?

LOUISE
It wasn't relevant, Sid.

SID
You lied to Mr. Bernbach?

LOUISE
My politics shouldn't matter.

SID
You're a Republican! How does that not matter?

LOUISE
Do you think I was going to pass on this because of my
voting record?

AARON
Are you telling me you'd vote for Goldwater?

LOUISE
No! Never! That's what I'm saying. What we just saw, those
people, that's not the Republican Party. Those are different
people. Goldwater's a different kind of man. I'm scared
of that man.

SID
And if Rockefeller was the nominee?

        Silence.

SID
Jesus, Lou.

LOUISE

You know you can count on me, Sid. You know Mr.
Bernbach can count on me.

SID

You've second-guessed every move we make.

LOUISE

I'm trying to make sure we do it right! Someone has to
consider the ramifications of what we're doing.

SID

What about the ramifications of losing the account? The
ramifications of getting fired! Have you thought about that?

AARON

Come on, Sid –

SID

(*speaking over*) God, you act like you're such an idealist.
Like you're the only one with real estate on the corner of
Ethics and Morality. But you're no better than anyone here,
and you know it!

AARON

Sid –

SID

If you think you're an idealist, you're deluded. No one
gets into this business that doesn't come out cynical. And
the only women in this racket who aren't cynics are the
secretaries. At least they can land husbands.

AARON

(*intervening*) Okay, Sid!

LOUISE
(*to* SID) Do you really think that hurts me? You don't
know me at all!

AARON
We've got bigger fish to fry than Louise's politics, alright?
I don't care who she votes for, so long as it's not Barry
Goldwater. We've got a board full of spots! "Social Security,"
"Eastern Seaboard," "Ice Cream," "Peace Little Girl." This is
an arsenal! Let's use it.

TONY
(*at the chalkboard*) What's this spot? "Peace Little Girl."
Is that new?

AARON
Oh, you're going to love this one, Tony! Lou
came up with it.

LOUISE
Aaron, wait –

AARON
It's very effective.

TONY
What is it?

AARON
Picture this. A little girl counts petals off a flower. One, two,
three. Then all of a sudden there's a countdown –

TONY
Are you serious?

AARON
Then: an explosion.

TONY

Yes, an explosion. I already know.

SID

What do you mean, you already know?

TONY

Because it's my spot.

LOUISE

It's from something Tony played for me. (*to TONY*) Sure, it's
based on that spot.

TONY

It's based on that spot, or it *is* that spot?

SID

(*to TONY*) Lou pitched it right in front of us.

TONY

From a spot I made two years ago.

LOUISE

It's a collaboration, Tony.

AARON

Of course it's a collaboration. And it's not like it's finished.
There's still all the details. Who's the girl? What's the
location? What kind of flower is she holding?

TONY & LOUISE

(*together*) A daisy.

SID

A daisy. Perfect.

AARON

How about a rose!

SID

    Enough talking. It's a hell of a spot. So let's get moving on it
    and get Clifford off our backs, alright?

AARON

    I know just the place we can shoot. And we need to do some
    casting. We need to find the perfect girl.

SID

    We need a script. A message. Lou, something about
    Goldwater's position on nukes.

AARON

    Maybe the quote about the Kremlin?

SID

    It's got to be tougher. Something that nails Barry to the wall.
    Like what he said about dropping low-yield nukes.

AARON

    Low-yield. Gimme a break.

TONY

    We don't mention Goldwater at all.

SID

    I'm sorry?

TONY

    We don't use his name.

SID

    What do you mean, don't use –

TONY

    We don't use Goldwater's name. We don't use Goldwater
    quotes. And we definitely don't show his face.

SID

Then how the hell is it about Goldwater?

TONY

Do you even understand how television works?

SID

Hey Tony, you're here to do sound, alright? If a sound issue comes up, we'll ask your advice.

AARON

Then let's put a plan together, huh? First things first, I'm ordering Chinese.

The telephone rings.

AARON

Oh, look. They're calling me. They're mind readers.

SID

Lou, let me run something by you.

SID pulls LOUISE over to the side.

TONY

(*answering the phone*) Hello?

AARON

So, guess which agency Goldwater hired? Leo Burnett.

SID

(*to LOUISE, discreet*) Listen to me. As far as I'm concerned, this spot was your idea. Not Tony's.

LOUISE

But Sid, the tape he played –

AARON

And guess who just started working for Leo Burnett.

TONY

(*on the phone*) Slow down, honey. What's happening?

AARON

Bob Thompson. Can you believe that?

SID

(*to LOUISE*) We don't know this guy. You want him to walk away from this with seven cents?

TONY

(*on the phone*) Sweetheart, I want you to get in a cab and come home. Right now.

> *He hangs up. Outside, police sirens can be heard approaching.*

LOUISE

Tony, what is it? Was that your wife?

TONY

(*nodding*) She's in Harlem. A police officer shot a young black kid. I think a riot just started.

ACT II | SCENE 2

The sidewalk outside TONY's studio, shortly after.

LOUISE has TONY's tape recorder over her shoulder, the microphone pointed into the night. As she moves from point to point, she records and bears witness to a city in chaos: sirens, shouts, windows smashing, children scared.

She enters TONY's studio, shaken. TONY is at his console, listening to a tape on headphones.

TONY
It sounds horrible out there.

LOUISE
It's worse up in Harlem. This is just the overspill. Johnson signed the Civil Rights Act a month ago, now we've got rioting on the streets.

TONY
Folks got tired of acting civil.

LOUISE
How's Reenah?

TONY
Shaken up, but she'll be fine.

LOUISE
How's the kid doing? The one who got shot?

TONY shakes his head.

LOUISE
This is going to get bad ... What are you listening to?

TONY
I was listening to you.

LOUISE
Me?

TONY
It's from what you said tonight. During the convention.
I made a little something.

LOUISE
(*suddenly worried*) What did you record?

> TONY *plays the tape. It's a recording of*
> LOUISE's *voice.*

LOUISE
(*recorded*) I grew up in a Republican house ... My father's
Republican. My family's Republican ... The first time I voted
was for Eisenhower in 1952 ... I voted for Richard Nixon
over Jack Kennedy ...

> LOUISE *quickly stops the tape.*

TONY
It's something I don't have much of. People's reactions to a
political event. I think it could be useful.

LOUISE
Oh, I'm sure you'll find a use for it.

TONY
What does that mean?

LOUISE
If Mr. Bernbach were to hear that tape ...

TONY

Why would I do that?

LOUISE

Why did you record it?

TONY

That's what I do ... We're friends, Louise.

LOUISE

I'm sorry. I'm a bit trigger happy. People can say all
they want about the collaborative nature of Doyle Dane
Bernbach, but it's still dog eat dog.

TONY

That's why I work on my own. That and the elevators.

LOUISE

Is that why you're no longer partners with that guy, Elliott?
Did it get competitive?

No answer.

LOUISE

It's none of my business. Forget I asked ... It's strange hearing me
talk about my father. We don't speak much. I should. His health
isn't good. Of course, he's more worried about me.

TONY

Why's that?

LOUISE

I didn't exactly turn out the way he hoped.

TONY

My parents are thrilled with how I turned out. It was their dream
to raise an agoraphobic hermit who runs around recording taxi
drivers ... How'd your father want you to turn out?

LOUISE

It's not even that I'm not married, and never likely will.
Or that I'll never make him a grandfather. It's that I took
what I was good at, what he was proud of, and now I
sell ketchup.

TONY

People need ketchup.

LOUISE

People need justice, Tony. Equality. World peace. Why aren't
I doing something about that?

TONY

Justice and equality, that's a tall order. As for world peace …

LOUISE

"Daisy"? … I think it's just going to scare people.

TONY

I'd say they're already scared.

> TONY *plays the tape* .

LOUISE

(*recorded*) What we just saw … That's not the Republican
Party … Goldwater's a different kind of man … I'm scared
of that man.

ACT II | SCENE 3

PROJECTION (text): August 4, 1964

CLIFFORD's office, the lights down low.

SID operates a slide projector. For every photo of black and white Americans in moments of peace and harmony, there's an image of the brutality of the day: riots and violence that have bloodied America's streets.

As the photos play, LOUISE narrates, reading from the speech that President Johnson delivered on July 2, 1964, announcing the signing of the Civil Rights Act.

CLIFFORD is seated.

LOUISE
(*reading*) "We believe that all men are created equal. Yet many are denied equal treatment. We believe that all men are entitled to the blessings of liberty. Yet millions are deprived of those blessings. We can understand – without rancour or hatred – how this all happened. But it cannot continue. The principles of our freedom forbid it. Morality forbids it. And the law I will sign tonight forbids it. Tonight, I urge every public official, every religious leader, every workingman, every housewife – I urge every American – to join in this effort to bring justice and hope to all our people, and to bring peace to our land."

SID
Vote for President Johnson on November 3rd.

The team looks to CLIFFORD.

SID

There you go, Cliff. That's a spot all ready to go. What do you think? (*no answer*) I know it wasn't on the menu, but it packs a punch, don't it?

CLIFFORD gets up and turns on the lights.

LOUISE

Right now, it's rough, but imagine it put together. You take the photos of the riots –

SID

Terrible.

LOUISE

Intercut with photos of the way things could be, the way things should be. You take Johnson's Civil Rights speech, you put that underneath ...

CLIFFORD takes a file from his desk.

SID

That's a spot, Cliff. That's a killer spot.

CLIFFORD

Tell me about this spot. Tell me about "Daisy."

SID

Sure, we can talk about "Daisy."

LOUISE

No. We need to focus on the Civil Rights spot.

SID

The man said he wants to hear about –

LOUISE
   This is real, Clifford. This is happening now. There are riots
   happening. We could see smoke from Jersey City on the
   train ride down.

AARON
   You got family involved, Cliff?

CLIFFORD
   What was that?

AARON
   In the riots. Any of your family affected?

CLIFFORD
   You said "involved."

AARON
   I mean, do you have family in the affected cities? New York.
   Rochester. Jersey City.

CLIFFORD
   No.

AARON
   But you know people involved, right?

CLIFFORD
   Are you serious?

LOUISE
   Aaron, for the love of –

AARON
   What?! I'm just asking if the guy knows people!

SID

Hey Aaron, I think they got one of those Automat vending machines upstairs.

AARON

Sure. Anyone want anything? (*getting no answer*)
I'll just be ...

AARON exits.

SID

So, Cliff, you like that script for "Daisy," huh? How's that storyboard? You wanted provocative. How's that for provocative?

CLIFFORD

I wanted a knockout punch. This is a gunshot to the face. I don't think I've ever seen anything like it. I'll take it to the President. Whose idea was "Daisy"?

LOUISE

(*hesitant*) It was mine. I'd been thinking about ... children ... and the power of numbers ... and how when you juxtapose them ... There were several influences.

CLIFFORD

Congratulations.

SID

(*unwilling to be left out*) My contribution's more in the visuals. This part here, where we zoom in, that's from a Truffaut film, *The 400 Blows*.

CLIFFORD

Let's see what else you have.

SID

We've got plenty!

LOUISE

We've got what we just showed you. The spot on the riots.
On Civil Rights. We can say something powerful. Something
hopeful. We can show how Johnson's been a champion for –

CLIFFORD

We're not going to make that spot.

LOUISE

Fine. If it's too strong, we can always soften –

CLIFFORD

We're not doing any spots on Civil Rights.

LOUISE

Why wouldn't we?

CLIFFORD

It's not a priority.

LOUISE

How can this not be a priority?

CLIFFORD

It's not a direction the President wants to take.

LOUISE

It's a direction the President needs to take.

CLIFFORD

And you're not here to set policy.

LOUISE

Do you know what they're calling the riots? Goldwater
Rallies. Blacks tearing up the streets? This is only helping
Goldwater's cause.

SID

Did you know Goldwater has supporters in the Klan?

CLIFFORD

You think Johnson doesn't have support he keeps under wraps? The man's from Texas.

SID

If you're taking "Daisy" to the President, Clifford, then why not take this to him as well?

CLIFFORD

I've already told you no.

LOUISE

Are you reading the same newspapers we're reading?

SID

Lou –

> LOUISE *grabs the slide projector controller and reverses back to several violent images.*

LOUISE

Six people were killed in the riots! People are dying over this!

CLIFFORD

Don't talk to me as if I don't know what's going on.

LOUISE

(*interrupting*) Do you?!

SID

Maybe we should –

LOUISE
I don't understand how the President won't speak about this!

CLIFFORD
(*interrupting*) Because he's keeping his distance from it.

LOUISE
Why would he do that?!

CLIFFORD
Because he needs a landslide!

LOUISE
(*after a moment*) The President's being silent because he might lose votes.

CLIFFORD
The riots are hurting him. Civil Rights is hurting him.

LOUISE
It's hurting him?!

CLIFFORD
He can't get his mandate if he doesn't win the South.

LOUISE
I don't believe this.

CLIFFORD
You ever spend much time with Southern Democrats, Miss Brown? See how they feel about Civil Rights down there. In politics, there's what's ideal and there's what's real.

AARON enters.

AARON
Guys!

CLIFFORD
If he doesn't get a majority, then all the progress he's made –

LOUISE
(*interrupting*) How is this progress?! Your own people are being killed!

CLIFFORD
(*interrupting*) I've walked down a road you haven't even stepped foot on, so don't you dare talk about race with me! Do you think there'd be a black man advising President Goldwater? I'd rather Lyndon Johnson, with all his faults, than any other white pretender!

AARON
Guys, we gotta –

LOUISE
(*right over AARON*) You're advertising for him. He's stashed you in the basement, and you're advertising for him.

AARON
We have to go!

SID
Aaron, it's not a good time –

AARON
(*interrupting*) You don't understand. Something's going on up there.

CLIFFORD *grabs the phone.*

AARON

    This guy came up and asked who I was. I said I was with
    Doyle Dane Bernbach. He just said we had to go. Now.

CLIFFORD

    (*on the phone*) Geraldine. What's happening?

AARON

    All the phones are ringing. There's military running up and
    down the corridor. Something's happened!

    CLIFFORD sits down in his chair.

CLIFFORD
    My God.

ACT II | SCENE 4

PROJECTION: Maps, film, and newsreel footage of the Gulf of Tonkin blend in with a mashed-up edit of PRESIDENT JOHNSON'S address on the Gulf of Tonkin attack.

PRESIDENT
(*on screen, out of sequence*) My fellow Americans ... Renewed hostile actions against the United States ships on the high seas in the Gulf of Tonkin ... It is my duty to the American people ... Attacking two destroyers with torpedoes ...

TONY's studio, later that night.
With the nation on high alert, SID, LOUISE, AARON and TONY listen to a recording of the President's remarks on a tape player.

AARON
This is bad. This is so bad.

SID
How many times are we going to listen to this?

PRESIDENT
(*recorded*) Air action is now in execution ...

AARON
See? Air action. You know what that means.

PRESIDENT
... against gunboats and certain supporting facilities in North Vietnam ...

LOUISE
He's sending in our bombers?

AARON
(*moving to telephone*) I'm calling Vera.

PRESIDENT
... Yet our response, for the present, will be limited and fitting ... I shall immediately request the Congress ...

AARON
Limited and fitting. Yeah, right.

PRESIDENT
... to pass a resolution to take all necessary measures ...

AARON
Come on, Vera. Pick up.

PRESIDENT
Such a resolution will be promptly introduced ...

AARON
(*on phone*) Vera, it's me. Wake up, sweetheart. How quick can you pack a bag?

SID
Geez, Aaron.

PRESIDENT
... freely and expeditiously debated ...

AARON
(*on phone*) Don't ask. Just pack some things.

PRESIDENT
... and passed with overwhelming support.

LOUISE
What does this mean?

AARON

(*on phone, as reassuring as possible*) Because we need to get to the bomb shelter.

SID

Calm down, Aaron.

PRESIDENT

It is my considered conviction ...

AARON

(*to SID*) Don't tell me to calm down!

PRESIDENT

... shared throughout your Government ...

AARON

(*speaking on phone*) I wasn't talking to you, Vera, but you should calm down, too.

PRESIDENT

... that firmness in the right is indispensable today for peace ...

AARON

(*speaking on phone*) I'll be home in fifteen minutes.

PRESIDENT

... That firmness will always be measured. Its mission is peace.

The President's address ends. AARON *hangs up the phone.*

AARON

Okay. I think I calmed down Vera.

SID

You woke her up in the middle of the night. She's a basket of nerves on a good day. I'm sure she's real calm now.

AARON

She's a wreck. This is bad. To make matters worse, what do I
tell her about the Secret Service?

SID

What about the Secret Service?

AARON

At the White House. One of them was giving me a look.

SID

What did you do, Aaron?

He pulls out an ashtray.

AARON

I took one of the White House ashtrays.

SID

Oh, for crying out loud!

LOUISE

Did we just go to war?

SID

Come on, Louise. Not you, too.

LOUISE

Is that what the President is saying?

SID

No one's said anything about war.

AARON

We sent over our bombers, Sid.

SID

Tony, play it back. Play the part about "limited and fitting."
We got attacked. It's a legitimate response.

TONY *plays back the tape.*

PRESIDENT

Our response, for the present, will be limited and fitting …
We still seek no wider war.

SID

See? "No wider war." Now let's get back to work.

AARON

You want to work now?!

LOUISE

He said our response, "for the present." What about next
week? Next month? … What about after the election?

SID

What do you mean, after?

LOUISE

We're creating a campaign on how a vote for Johnson is a
vote for peace. But a half-rate navy throws a few torpedoes,
and we're sending in our bombers? Are we provoking a war?

SID

We're not provoking anything! Lyndon Johnson is a
responsible man. If that was Goldwater he'd have the nukes
on the table. That's what we should be focused on. Keeping a
warmonger from becoming President.

LOUISE

I hope we don't already have one.

Everything stops.

SID
Now you wait a goddamn second.

LOUISE
You're not the least bit –

SID
(*interrupting*) Watch your mouth, Republican! You got one strike when you lied to me.

LOUISE
I had every right –

SID
(*pushing through*) You just called my President a warmonger. That's two.

LOUISE
Sid –

SID
You want to swing that bat again? ... Dammit, we're not politicians! We're here to make ads. Can we make the goddamn ads! Aaron, I want to shoot Louise's ad this week. I want "Daisy" in the can.

TONY
So we're calling "Daisy" Louise's ad?

SID
Oh, look. He speaks.

TONY
Why are you calling it Louise's ad?

SID
Does none of what we're saying matter to you?

LOUISE
Sid –

TONY
It's from my idea.

SID
You weren't there when Lou pitched it.

TONY
Which she couldn't have done if it weren't for a spot I made
two years ago.

AARON
(*interrupting*) No one's saying you didn't contribute, Tony.

TONY
No one's saying I did, either!

SID
And you're under contract with Doyle Dane Bernbach. Read
your contract!

LOUISE
Sid, would you stop? Tony, no one's stealing anything. We all
made it. If it plays good, we all look good. But if it plays
bad – and it could play bad – we all come out tainted.

SID
I'm tired of talking about it! Let's get the goddamn thing
made. Aaron, what do we got?

AARON
(*with his black book*) We got the location. We got the
crew. We got our little Daisy Girl, cute as a button.
We're ready to shoot.

SID

    All we need is a script. We need to know what we're saying about Goldwater.

TONY

    No!

SID

    Tony –

TONY

    For the last time: no!

SID

    It's an anti-Goldwater ad and we don't even name him!

TONY

    His name is already there!

SID

    Where?

TONY

    Inside the audience! Before we even show the commercial! "Daisy" will work when it makes people recall what Goldwater already said!

SID

    Tony, the spot needs a message to make people afraid of how –

TONY

    (*interrupting*) We don't need to make people afraid! They're already afraid! They're afraid Goldwater could start a nuclear war! The message is already there!

LOUISE

    Finally! Someone admits it. "Daisy" is about fear.

TONY

No, Louise.

LOUISE

Yes. We are making a commercial that exploits fear. That creates fear.

TONY

It's not *creating* anything.

LOUISE

We are deliberately manipulating –

SID

That's it, I've had it! I'm done! You need a goddamn psychology degree to work with the two of you! I am not a manipulator! I'm here to fight, alright? Politics is ugly. It's dirty and it's ugly. I'm just doing my goddamn job!

LOUISE

Sid –

SID exits.

LOUISE

He's just going to leave?

AARON

I'll talk to him. I should go, too. It's late. I should be with Vera. (*to LOUISE*) I really hope you're wrong. About the President. I hope we're both wrong.

AARON exits.

LOUISE

(*after a moment*) What are we doing? What am I doing? The things I'm saying. The things I'm creating. It's all so … cynical.

TONY
What is?

LOUISE
Everything. Me. "Daisy". All of it.

TONY
"Daisy" is not cynical.

TONY loads a tape onto a machine.

LOUISE
You think "Daisy" is optimistic?

TONY
It's neither. It's about what's true. Cynicism or optimism
have no bearing. As for you, the jury's still out.

LOUISE
And who's the jury?

TONY
You are.

*He plays the tape. It's a continuation of a tape he
played earlier.*

SOUND: A puppy barking.

LOUISE
Tony ...

NARRATOR
(*on tape*) Tony was passed on to an attendant who took him
downstairs ...

LOUISE
Tony, if you don't mind.

NARRATOR
… to the room where the dogs were quartered. On the way Tony explained that he was looking for a nice, quiet, ordinary dog.

Multiple dogs barking.

LOUISE
Now's not a good time!

TONY turns off the machine.

TONY
The man who wrote that committed suicide in front of me.

LOUISE
(*after a moment*) What?

TONY
I used to think Elliott was cynical, but that's not what it was. He had depression. But I didn't see it. I didn't see what was already there. Elliott was separating from his wife. There were money problems. He was saying some pretty dark things … There was this party one night. He didn't want to go. I told him we should both go, that he needed to cheer up. For both our sakes. Elliott was not an easy person to work with. It's not like I wanted to go to a party: it was ten blocks from here, it was on the sixth floor … They were playing jazz. Elliott loved jazz. I told him to mingle. He had a few drinks, but he wouldn't talk to anybody. He wasn't having a good time. I said let's go. We went to get our coats in the bedroom … We were in the room. I was thanking the host. And then Elliott made this *sound.* I looked over. He threw his coat onto the floor. Then his wallet. He ran to the window. And then he was gone.

LOUISE
Elliott was your partner.

TONY

And despite his many failings, I liked working with him. I miss it … I like working with you, Louise.

LOUISE

You don't have to worry about me. I'm not depressed.

TONY

It's not your mental state that concerns me. It's your uncertainty. You have to believe in what we're doing.

LOUISE

I'm trying.

TONY

Try harder. "Daisy" is about peace. It's about saving us all. It's going to be the most positive message ever created.

Darkness. Then as the scene transitions: we hear the voice of a television DIRECTOR, *coaching a young* GIRL *into the history books.*

DIRECTOR

(*recorded*) Now you lift up the flowers, honey. All the way. All the way. Now turn and look this way. Just turn. That's it. Just a little bit. Now come back this way, honey. Just to me. Honey, this way. Alright. Now start picking the flower. "One." Real loud.

DAISY GIRL

(*recorded*) 1 … 2 … 3 …

ACT II | SCENE 5

The work room at Doyle Dane Bernbach. Late.

LOUISE sits at her desk, with a drink. The film projector plays a commercial.

PROJECTION: In the commercial, "Confessions of a Republican," a stern-looking REPUBLICAN speaks to the camera.

REPUBLICAN
(*on screen*) I don't know just why they wanted to call this a confession. I certainly don't feel guilty about being a Republican. I've always been a Republican. My father is. His father was. The whole family is a Republican family. I voted for Dwight Eisenhower the first time I ever voted. I voted for Nixon the last time.

BERNBACH enters.

REPUBLICAN
But when we come to Senator Goldwater, now it seems to me we're up against a very different kind of man. This man scares me.

BERNBACH turns off the machine.

BERNBACH
You're working late.

LOUISE
So are you.

LOUISE takes out the bottle and another glass and pours BERNBACH a drink.

BERNBACH
The Democratic convention's on television. I thought
I'd watch it here. I just listened to the President accept
the nomination.

LOUISE
I caught the beginning.

BERNBACH
I trust that drink's in celebration.

LOUISE
Let's hope so.

BERNBACH
(*raising his glass*) To Lyndon Johnson.

LOUISE
To paying the bills.

She finishes her drink.

LOUISE
Mr. Bernbach, there's something I need to tell you.

BERNBACH
I know you're a Republican, Louise. (*off her reaction*) Insight
into human nature is part of the communicator's skill.

LOUISE
Then why'd you put me on the account?

BERNBACH
Because the White House can't tell me who I can and can't
put on an account. I put you on because you're the best
writer here.

LOUISE

What if I'd said I was Republican?

BERNBACH

But you didn't. Ambition is a great enabler. It breeds creativity. (*referring to the projector*) This one here? A brilliant piece of writing. And as for "Daisy" ...

LOUISE

I hear you showed it to the President.

BERNBACH

I did. We watched it together.

LOUISE

Did he have anything to say about it?

BERNBACH

The President wasn't happy with the quality of his voice ... "Daisy" has been approved, Louise. It's going to play.

LOUISE

Mr. Bernbach, you realize that once we open that box, I don't know if it can be closed.

BERNBACH

But that's who we are, Louise. People like you and I, we're the shapers of society. We can vulgarize it. We can brutalize it. Or, once in a career, maybe once in a lifetime, we can lift it to a higher level.

LOUISE

And are we lifting it to a higher level?

BERNBACH

It was fascinating, listening to the President. In the political arena, the man is a gladiator. He told me that when it comes to elections, each side is convinced that the other is so depraved they pose a genuine threat to our very survival. And since it's impossible to get people who think like that to switch sides, since it's easier to provoke voters than to educate them, it all comes down to getting the people who do support you to just show up and vote. The man who wins is the one who can generate the most hope or fear.

LOUISE
I don't know if what we're doing is right.

BERNBACH
That hasn't stopped you from being good at it. I trust you'll continue – as Head Copywriter.

BERNBACH leaves.

Darkness. Then as the scene transitions:

PROJECTION (text): September 7, 1964, 9:45 p.m.

The moment has arrived. The commercial is about to play. Everyone is present to witness it: AARON, SID, BERNBACH, TONY, CLIFFORD, and LOUISE.

PROJECTION: The commercial plays. It begins with the sound of birds, as the young, innocent DAISY GIRL plucks petals from a flower.

DAISY GIRL
(*on screen*) 1 ... 2 ... 3 ... 4 ... 5 ... 7 ... 6 ... 6 ... 8 ... 9 ... 9 ...

The voice of a countdown begins. The camera closes in on the GIRL's eye.

COUNTDOWN
(*recorded*) 10... 9 ... 8 ... 7 ... 6 ... 5... 4 ... 3... 2 ... 1 ... 0!

An atomic explosion is detonated inside the girl's
eye. As the fires of hell are unleashed, PRESIDENT
JOHNSON *soberly intones:*

PRESIDENT
(*recorded*) These are the stakes. To make a world in which
all of God's children can live, or to go into the dark. We must
either love each other, or we must die.

ANNOUNCER
(*recorded*) Vote for President Johnson on November 3rd.
The stakes are too high for you to stay home.

Static fills the screen.

ACT II | SCENE 6

The work room at Doyle Dane Bernbach.
A week later.

SID and AARON read through a stack of letters.
LOUISE sits apart.

SID

(*reading from a letter*) "... and in closing, please accept
my gratitude. My party made a big mistake in nominating
the fear-monger Barry Goldwater, and I can no longer
support that man."

AARON

Amen to that!

SID

You hear that, Lou? One more vote for the good guys.

AARON

(*reading from a different letter*) "I was sad to learn that your
commercial will no longer be broadcast. As far as I can tell,
it's Goldwater who should be taken off the air!"

SID

(*to LOUISE*) You hear that, kiddo? We did that. Johnson's up
six points in one week.

AARON

Here's another one. "Dear Mr. Bernbach, please
commend your team."

SID

Six points! (*to AARON*) Hey, what time are we
talking to CBS?

AARON

Four o'clock. (*continues reading*) "The advertisement with the little girl was a remarkable achievement ..." You hear that? Remarkable. "... in political blasphemy. You have raised the bar in your ability to manipulate ..." Oh, I see. This one's not so good.

SID

You can't please them all.

AARON

"I was so disgusted by what I witnessed on television that I had to turn it off, which was frustrating, considering it's my first television."

SID

What's important is Johnson's up six points, and that people know we made it happen.

AARON

"What gives you the right to kill that little girl?" Geez, it's not like she didn't get paid.

SID

Lou, you should read some of these. Bask in the glory.

LOUISE

It doesn't sound very glorious.

SID

What did Vera make of "Daisy"? She telling everyone what a big shot her husband is?

AARON

Vera moved in with her mother.

LOUISE

What?

AARON
She didn't like the ad very much. She was pretty scared.
She got angry.

LOUISE
Oh, Aaron.

AARON
She's sensitive. She'll be back.

SID
(*holding a letter*) Hey, this one's from a politician.

LOUISE
Who?

SID
Chairman of the Republican National Committee.

LOUISE
Are you serious?

SID
"I am hereby entering a formal complaint. This horror-type
commercial has no place in this or any campaign."

AARON
(*holding another letter*) This one's from a Senator. "This
commercial has taken political campaigning to a depth never
before approached in the history of television." At least we're
making history.

        LOUISE takes the letter.

LOUISE
"The use of fear to avoid an honest discussion should not be
tolerated. I know of one child who had nausea all night."

SID

Then don't let your kid watch television.

LOUISE

You find this funny? Are you listening at all? Don't you understand what we've done?

SID

Yeah, we crushed Barry Goldwater. We did good. Why else would we be doing all these interviews? I'm telling you, I don't know how I'll go back to straight advertising!

LOUISE

We killed a little girl on national television! We're the fear-mongers!

AARON picks up another envelope.

SID

Funny, I don't recall you looking away when Cliff asked who made "Daisy." I don't recall you turning down Bernbach's offer to become Head Copywriter.

AARON

Hey, Lou. You might want to see this one.

LOUISE

No, I don't.

AARON

I think you do.

LOUISE takes the envelope. She sees who it's sent from. She pulls out a letter.

SID

Listen, Lou, we've got to stop butting heads. We've got the makings of something big here. Let's put the past in the past, and let bygones be bygones. (*no answer*) What is it?

LOUISE grabs her coat and leaves.

SID

What's that all about?

AARON

A whole lot of past and bygones.

ACT II | SCENE 7

TONY's studio, shortly after.

TONY sits at his console, reviewing a contract. As he does so, he also listens to the soundtrack for "Ice Cream," another commercial created by the team from Doyle Dane Bernbach.

FEMALE NARRATOR
(*recorded*) Do you know what people used to do? They used to explode atomic bombs in the air. Now children should have lots of Vitamin A and Calcium, but they shouldn't have any strontium-90 or cesium-137.

LOUISE enters.

FEMALE NARRATOR
These things come from atomic bombs, and they're radioactive. They can make you die.

LOUISE turns off the track.

TONY
That's the first time a woman narrated a political commercial. It's historic ... Is there something I can do for you, Louise?

LOUISE
Convince me that what we did wasn't wrong.

TONY
Wrong?

LOUISE
With "Daisy." With what we did. "The most positive message ever created."

TONY
What's this about?

LOUISE
I think you're brilliant, Tony. I really do. But you're so naive.

TONY
I think you should –

LOUISE
(*interrupting*) And the sad thing is I want to believe in you.
I want to believe in Mr. Bernbach. But the one person I've
always believed in just made it absolutely clear how wrong
this all is.

TONY
(*interrupting*) I don't know what ...

LOUISE
My father wrote me a letter! ... After he saw "Daisy,"
he wrote to tell me just how disappointed–

CLIFFORD enters. He's got a sandwich.

CLIFFORD
So, Tony, have I got a story to tell you about ... Miss Brown.
What a nice surprise.

LOUISE
Did we have a meeting scheduled?

CLIFFORD
We did not. I came up to take care of some other business
with Tony, whose wife makes an excellent sandwich.

LOUISE
What other business?

CLIFFORD

You should hear this story, too. I know you'll appreciate
it. So, it's the night "Daisy" played. It's around ten o'clock.
My phone rings. It's the President. The man is not pleased.
He's got friends over. They've all just watched it. (*to* TONY)
What's that spice?

TONY

Lemon pepper.

CLIFFORD

Lemon pepper. (*continuing the story*) So the President gets
me on the phone. "What the hell were you thinking, Cliff?
You get over here and tell me what you plan to do about
this." (*pointing to contract*) The terms for payment are on the
third page. (*continuing the story*) So I run, and I mean run
to the residence. The President rips into me. Right in front
of his guests. "What the hell are those Madison Avenue
boys thinking?" All I can say is "But it only played once, sir.
We'll take it off the air." "Well, Cliff, you make damn sure it
doesn't play again. Not even Barry Goldwater deserves this."
So, I turn and head out. I'm sure I'm on a bus first thing in
the morning. "Hold on a minute, Cliff." The President strides
down the hall. Comes right up and puts his big ol' hand on
my shoulder. (*whispering*) "So Cliff, you sure we ought to
run it just the one time?"

LOUISE

(*after a moment*) Why are you meeting with Tony and
not all of us?

CLIFFORD

Because this isn't about the current campaign, Miss Brown.
There's mid-terms in two years. Another presidential election
in four. I've got my eye on the future.

LOUISE
Are you serious?

TONY signs the contract.

LOUISE
(*to* TONY) You've signed on to this? (*to* CLIFFORD)
You're under contract with Doyle Dane Bernbach. There's a
renewal clause –

CLIFFORD
Which no longer stands since the contract's in breach.

LOUISE
How is it in breach?

CLIFFORD
Because Bernbach put a Republican on the account.

LOUISE
(*to* TONY) You told him?

CLIFFORD
No, Miss Brown, I did my job. I had my doubts about you
from day one. So, I did some digging. And up came Robert
Brown, of Lancaster, Ohio. Registered Republican, and
father of Louise Brown.

LOUISE
Mr. Bernbach shouldn't be faulted for what I did. As a
professional courtesy, you owe him –

CLIFFORD
Speaking of courtesy, remind me how you came up with
"Daisy." It was something about children, and numbers, and
how they're juxtaposed ... Tony played me the tape "Daisy"
came from. He played me a lot of tapes.

TONY

Do you know how many articles I've read about "Daisy"?
A lot. I'm not mentioned in any of them.

LOUISE

What do you want me to say?

CLIFFORD

You can admit you took credit for something you didn't
make, don't believe in, and quite likely never understood.
Tony understands all of this better than you and I and
everyone put together. And from where I'm standing, all
of this is all that matters. Who cares about speeches and
slogans? Tony's found a way to grab us by the guts. It's the
new politics.

LOUISE

The new politics ... We made it a strategy not to put the
President in his own goddamn ads. We made it a strategy
to be unrelentingly combative. We reduced the national
discourse to blowing up a little girl. Is that the new politics?

CLIFFORD

It is if it wins. (*picking up the contract*) The President looks
forward to meeting you, Tony.

TONY

He'll have to come here. I'm not getting on a train.

LOUISE

What kind of Great Society will it be if the President has to
scare us into getting there?

CLIFFORD

By and by, Miss Brown. By and by.

CLIFFORD *leaves.*

LOUISE

    I guess you're proud.

TONY

    And you aren't?

      TONY pulls out a newspaper.

TONY

    "The team of Aaron Ehrlich, Sid Myers, and Louise Brown work collaboratively. None could remember who came up with the idea for the little girl and the daisy. 'It was a team effort,' said Miss Brown." That's from *The New York Times*.

LOUISE

    That's not what matters right now –

TONY

    It's all that matters! ... I thought we could have been partners. I have nothing to say to you.

LOUISE

    Yes, you do. You just signed a pact to sink us deeper into this mess. We gave them their weapon, Tony! They're going to take what we made and –

TONY

    What *I* made! ... "Daisy" worked because it reflected what people knew about Goldwater. It reflected the truth! If you can't see the good in that ... if you can't see that what I do can *only* be used for good –

LOUISE

    There's your problem, Tony. You're an optimist. You've got too much faith in people.

TONY

    And you don't have enough.

LOUISE
    Well, call me a cynic, but you only know eight blocks'
    worth of people.

TONY
    And none of them betrayed me.

ACT II | SCENE 8

> *LOUISE watches news footage on television.*

> *PROJECTION: Walter Cronkite announces the election results on CBS.*

CRONKITE
(*on screen*) Lyndon Baines Johnson has been elected President of the United States. And the landslide has carried him in for his first term in office on his own right by his own election.

> *The footage ends with music: "Hail to the Chief."*

ACT II | SCENE 9

PROJECTION (*text*): April 1965

PROJECTION: Full-color film footage of Operation Rolling Thunder, the U.S. Air Force bombing campaign of North Vietnam.

The lobby of New York's Lincoln Center Philharmonic. Beyond the lobby doors, an awards gala is underway.

EMCEE
(*heard from the auditorium*) And the winner of the Distinctive Merit Award is Doyle Dane Bernbach.

Applause.

EMCEE
Named on the award are Bill Bernbach, creative director; Louise Brown, copywriter ...

LOUISE enters from the auditorium, dressed for a gala. She starts across the lobby, heading for the exit.

EMCEE
... Sid Myers, art director; and Aaron Ehrlich, producer. Accepting the award is Bill Bernbach.

BERNBACH enters from the auditorium, dressed in a tuxedo.

BERNBACH
Louise!

EMCEE
Oh, my mistake.

LOUISE

No, Mr. Bernbach, I shouldn't have come.

EMCEE

Accepting the award is Sid Myers.

BERNBACH

Louise, stop.

LOUISE

I'm not accepting it. I won't. I'm going home.

BERNBACH

You're not going home. You're going to get back in that
room. There are photographers, reporters, a room full of –

LOUISE

You want me to talk to reporters? Fine! I'll talk to reporters.

BERNBACH

Now you listen to me –

LOUISE

It's about time someone says something!

BERNBACH

Do not get in the way of my legacy! Now, I'm asking you,
with as much consideration as I can, to get back in that
room, put on a goddamn smile, and accept your award.

LOUISE

I will not. And I don't understand how, in good
conscience, you can.

BERNBACH

Don't confuse the respect I have for you with
patience, Louise.

LOUISE

Don't assume the respect I have for you comes without limits.

> *Applause.* SID *and* AARON *enter from the auditorium.* SID*'s got an award statue.* AARON*'s got two.*

SID

There you both are. You didn't come up with us. (*to* BERNBACH) I only spoke, Mr. Bernbach, because you didn't go up.

BERNBACH

Yes. Thank you, Sidney.

AARON

(*holding up the statues*) Look at these. Ain't they beauties? Here's yours, Lou.

> *He gives* LOUISE *her award.*

AARON

I left yours with Vera, Mr. Bernbach.

BERNBACH

That's fine.

AARON

I warn you, she's got a pretty strong grip. She sure is happy now! A campaign for the ages, huh? I'm getting misty-eyed. Which is very painful. Vera's got my drops. I'll see you back in there.

> AARON *heads back in.*

SID

They want to take a group photo. You two coming?

BERNBACH
Give us a minute.

SID
Sure ... We did good work, didn't we ... Hey, kiddo, here's
that money I owe you.

> SID *places some money in* LOUISE's *hand, then*
> *heads back in.*

BERNBACH
You'd think I pay him enough not to borrow. How much
did he owe?

LOUISE
(*looking in her hands*) Seven cents.

BERNBACH
You deserve that award.

LOUISE
And I wanted it. I worked for it. God, I even stole for it. But
when I heard that announcer say our name, say my name,
as acknowledgment for something so ...

BERNBACH
Louise –

LOUISE
And to be reminded of it every night on television as the
bombs fall ...

BERNBACH
Fine. It's a bittersweet victory. Is that what you want to hear?
I never presumed that Lyndon Johnson is perfect. He may
not be the man, he may not be the peacemaker we made him
out to be, but I'll take a month of bombing over what Barry
Goldwater might have done any day.

LOUISE

That's some legacy.

BERNBACH

We got a president elected. We fundamentally changed the landscape of advertising.

LOUISE

You're damn right we did.

BERNBACH

(*after a moment*) It's fascinating to watch you agonize over a self-inflicted wound. Your name is on that award because your ambition is stronger than your ideals. And that's life. When you get to my age, you'll see that the best we can do is make choices for an imperfect world. If you don't believe me, call your father and ask him. (*turning to go*) Good night, Louise.

LOUISE

My father and I, we used to listen to debates. He had a hardware store, and he'd play the debates on the radio he kept behind the counter. Didn't matter what election. Presidential, governors. We listened to them all.

BERNBACH

I'm not looking to debate you, Louise.

LOUISE

He died last month … He loved debates. He loved politics. The man never finished high school, but the respect he had … for discourse … When we listened to them, I kept score on this little chalkboard. You got two points for landing a solid argument. You lost two for cheap sentiment. He'd boo if you tried to duck a question. And if you lied? He'd be done with you. We even debated each other. Customers loved it. People came in just to hear the two of us argue. I thought he was angry. But he was proud … He wanted me to go into politics.

I said women don't make it there. He said the only thing that mattered was integrity, and that I had it in spades ... When I got this job, the first thing I did was tell him that I was working for Bill Bernbach. And that I was good at it. That I could do good ... When he saw "Daisy," when he saw what I'd done, he wrote to tell me that he never thought he could be so disappointed ... Which is nothing compared to how much I disappointed myself.

She hands him the award.

LOUISE
Good night, Mr. Bernbach.

She leaves.

ACT II | SCENE 10

TONY gives a lecture in his studio.

TONY
If you could take a vessel, if there was a way to contain all
of the anxiety pressing down upon us at this particular
moment, what would you do with that mass, once you
beheld its impossible size? The optimists among us might
believe that it will subside with time. The cynics likely fear it
never will. But the pragmatist sees it for what it is: an anxiety
that is simply there ... After "Daisy" aired, there was as much
praise as there was criticism. But to say that it was negative?
That it was manipulative? When the audience participates
in the message, when the audience *is* the message, how is
that manipulation? ... A philosopher once said, "I think;
therefore, I am." But someone inside a voting booth is
more likely to say, "I feel; therefore, I choose." I can't create
sadness, or fear. I can't create love, or hope. I can only work
with what already exists in us. And I have tremendous belief
in what exists in us.

TONY plays a tape: the sound of a heartbeat.

END OF PLAY.

Acknowledgments

My playwriting is influenced by numerous collaborators: theatre artists, real-life interview subjects, my wife. I'm easily
persuaded by ideas better than my own. One of those ideas
came from Valerie Sing Turner, a passionate advocate for equity
and diversity in Canadian theatre. Valerie was aware of my new
play, and that its characters were all-white, and all-male, which
reflected the real-life people who were being depicted. Valerie
challenged me to break my own mould. At first, I resisted. And
then, Stan Lee became Louise Brown, a strong woman's voice in
an environment dominated by men. And Lloyd Wright became
Clifford Lewis, a black man navigating multiple conflicts in
white America. And the play is better for it.

Back in 2012, when *Daisy* was not much more than a synopsis on
a page, I asked fellow Canadian playwright Kevin Kerr for a letter
of support for a grant application. Kevin's letter was fantastic,
and I'm certain it helped secure some of those early grants. But
within Kevin's letter was his own twenty-five-word encapsulation
of what *Daisy* was about: themes and context, neatly presented
in one well-scripted sentence. In other words, a guide.

For their much more direct contributions, I wish to acknowledge
the following people and institutions, whose insight, experience,
and generosity were invaluable in the research and development
of this play: John Langs and ACT Theatre, Anton Schwartz,
Sid Myers, John Carey, Kathleen Hall Jamieson, Bill Geerhart,
Robert Spero, Allen Fitzpatrick and the Icicle Creek New Play
Festival, Horseshoes & Hand Grenades Theatre, Kirsten Potter,
Michael Gotch, Tré Cotten, R. Hamilton Wright, Connor
Toms, Bradford Farwell, the Tony Schwartz Collection at the
Library of Congress, Ensemble Studio Theatre and the Alfred
P. Sloan Foundation, William Bogert, Michael Rowan, David

Hoffman, Reena Schwartz, Kayla Schwartz, Kathleen Gordon and DDB New York, Don Blauweiss, Chuck Schroeder, the Canada Council for the Arts, the Ontario Arts Council, and the City of Ottawa.

I also wish to credit the Democratic National Committee for allowing the use of and reference to the "Daisy" commercial and all other DNC commercials from the 1964 campaign.

To my many, many collaborators, thanks.

Notes

Page 4: Several of Tony Schwartz's monologues are based on actual writings and recordings by the real Tony Schwartz, including segments from his book *The Responsive Chord: How radio and TV manipulate you ... who you vote for ... what you buy ... and how you think* (Garden City, NY: Anchor Press, 1973).

Page 4: Tony Schwartz's speech – "If there's a subject I can speak about with some level of expertise, it would be the area of sound" – is based on a Schwartz video lecture called "The Power of Audio with Tony Schwartz," which was produced by David Hoffman. This video lecture also contains a segment of a recording that Tony Schwartz produced of voice actor Bob Landers: "Long before you could see the difference between a smile or a frown, you could hear the difference in the sound of a word. In the sound of anger. The sound of love. The sound of fear." The clip is taken from *Guerilla Media* (Princeton, NJ : Films for the Humanities & Sciences, 1989), VHS. To view the video lecture, see: https://youtu.be/o_HGBsinKdY

Page 5: Tony Schwartz refers to an experiment on "the nature of silence," based on an experiment by composer John Cage. To view video of Cage describing the experiment, which is a clip from *Global Groove*, directed by Nam June Paik and John Godfrey (1973; NY: Electronic Arts Intermix, 2012), DVD, see: https://youtu.be/jS9ZOlFB-kI

Page 41: The stage directions refer to *The Horse in Motion* (1878), a film by Eadweard Muybridge. The film, also known as *Sallie Gardner*, may be found at the Library of Congress website, as well as other sites.

Page 48: To hear the "Come to Bufferin" radio commercial created by Tony Schwartz, as well as the "Come to Mama" alternative experiment, refer to "Media Samples" at: http://horseshoesandhandgrenades.ca/past-projects/daisy/

Page 54: Clifford Lewis listens to "The Great Society Speech," delivered by President Lyndon Johnson to the University of Michigan on May 22, 1964. To hear this part of the speech, refer to segment 2:47–3:43 at: https://youtu.be/x4Qc1VM80aQ (for a full transcript of the speech, refer to The American Presidency Project at UC Santa Barbara website: http://www.presidency.ucsb.edu/ws/?pid=26262).

Page 61: To view "Bus Driver" (1952), the political commercial, refer to: http://www.livingroomcandidate.org/commercials/1952/bus-driver. See other citations in this list for other commercials on the www. livingroomcandidate.org website.

Page 69: To hear the Tony Schwartz track called "Ring Games" and other tracks from the album *1, 2, 3 and a Zing Zing Zing* (Washington, DC: Smithsonian Folkways, 2007, 1953), refer to: http://www.folkways. si.edu/tony-schwartz/1-2-3-and-a-zing-zing-zing/childrens/music/ album/smithsonian

Page 70: Tony Schwartz plays part of a track from the recording *An Actual Story in Sound of a Dog's Life* (Washington, DC: Smithsonian Folkways, 2004, 1958). The segment he plays, from "Dog's Life, Part I," may be heard at: http://www.folkways.si.edu/tony-schwartz/an-actual-story-in-sound-of-a-dogs-life/childrens-documentary-miscellany/ album/smithsonian

Page 75: To hear the Schwartz radio commercial "Sometimes" (1962), refer to: http://conelrad.com/daisy/audio.php . The www.conelrad. com/daisy website is a marvelous overall reference for further study.

Page 95: The characters watch footage of Governor Nelson Rockefeller at the 1964 Republican National Convention. To view the specific footage being described, refer to segment 5:40–6:50 at: http://www.c-span.org/video/?c3807346/governor-nelson-rockefeller-addresses-64-convention

Page 98: The characters watch footage of Senator Barry Goldwater at the 1964 Republican National Convention. To view the specific footage being described, refer to segment 43:49–45:07 at: https://www.c-span.org/video/?4018-1/barry-goldwater-accepts-1964-republican-presidential-nomination

Page 113: Louise Brown quotes from the speech delivered by President Lyndon Johnson on July 2, 1964, commemorating the signing of the Civil Rights Act. To hear the speech and view a transcript, refer to: https://www.loc.gov/exhibits/civil-rights-act/multimedia/ johnson-signing-remarks.html

Page 122: The characters listen to a recording of President Lyndon Johnson delivering the historic Report on the Tonkin Gulf Incident on August 4, 1964. To view footage of this televised address, refer to: https://youtu.be/Dx8-ffiYyzA

Page 133: To hear footage of the film crew during the recording of the actual "Daisy" commercial in 1964, refer to: http://conelrad.com/daisy/audio.php

Page 134: To view the political commercial "Confessions of a Republican" (1964), refer to: http://www.livingroomcandidate.org/commercials/1964/confessions-of-a-republican

Page 137: To view the political commercial "Peace, Little Girl (Daisy)" (1964), refer to: http://www.livingroomcandidate.org/commercials/1964/peace-little-girl-daisy

Page 144: To view the political commercial "Ice Cream" (1964), refer to: http://www.livingroomcandidate.org/commercials/1964/ice-cream

Page 151: The characters listen to television footage of CBS News anchor Walter Cronkite calling the election victory for President Lyndon Johnson on November 3, 1964. To view the footage, go to segment 1:45:35– 1:45:48 of: https://youtu.be/aOkwpqlOQgo

SEAN DEVINE is a Canadian playwright, actor, and artistic director of Horseshoes & Hand Grenades Theatre. His most recent play *Daisy* premiered at Seattle's A Contemporary Theatre (ACT) in 2016, where it received a Gregory Award nomination for Outstanding New Play and a Broadway World Seattle Critic's Choice Award for Best New Play. Originally commissioned by NYC's Ensemble Studio Theatre, *Daisy* has had public readings in Chicago, Toronto, and Ottawa. Devine's first play *Re:Union* premiered in Vancouver in 2011, was published by Scirocco in 2013, and was presented at Ottawa's Magnetic North Theatre Festival in 2015, where it won the Prix Rideau Award for Ottawa's Best Production. Devine's newest play, *When There's Nothing Left to Burn*, was commissioned by the University of Lethbridge, where it premiered in 2017. Devine lives in Ottawa with his wife Alexa and their four kids. He ran for federal office as the NDP candidate for Nepean in the 2015 election. He lost.